The New England

GALAXY

Scene in Old Sturbridge Village *(photo by James C. Ward)*

The New England GALAXY

edited by

ROGER PARKS

*The best of 20 years from
Old Sturbridge Village*

CHESTER · CONNECTICUT

© 1980 Old Sturbridge, Inc.
ISBN: 0–87106–040–x
Library of Congress Catalog Number: 80–66598
Manufactured in the United States of America
First Edition

INTRODUCTION

"New England is wrote upon my heart in as strong characters as Calais was upon Queen Mary's," wrote Thomas Hutchinson, the former royal governor of Massachusetts, from exile during the American Revolution. New England is a place and New Englanders a people who have always evoked strong feelings. Some observers have found New England's people as forbidding as its climate and terrain. Others, like the late novelist David C. DeJong, Dutch by birth and a New Englander by choice, have discovered that beneath its stony surface the region is "receptive to all who understand its peculiar dignity."

DeJong's article, "What Is This about New England?" is one of 23 in this volume that examine the peculiar dignity and some of the just plain peculiarities of New England and its people. Most of the stories deal with incidents, experiences and characters from the past; a few look at New England today, emphasizing roles that the past still plays. All appeared in *The New-England Galaxy*, a quarterly magazine of regional history, published for 20 years by Old Sturbridge Village until rising costs forced an end to publication in 1979. Ably edited by Catherine Fennelly, the *Galaxy* circulated mainly to members of the Village, the well known, outdoor museum of New England history in Sturbridge, Massachusetts. This book makes some of the stories available to a wider audience for the first time.

Old Sturbridge Village recreates everyday life in a small, inland community during the early decades of the nineteenth century. A number of the articles here focus on that period in New England's history—a time of great social, economic and intellectual ferment. Most people in this volume, like those whose lives the Village portrays, are nearly forgotten today, though some achieved notoriety by one means or another in their own day. Whether they lived by, exceeded or threatened community norms, the people described here were mostly strong characters—that is, New Englanders. They appear on these pages for the enjoyment of all who feel strongly about New England.

Roger Parks
Old Sturbridge Village

May 1980

TABLE OF CONTENTS

The True Country Auction

by Lorna Beers

If you spend your summer holiday driving along the back roads and through the isolated villages of Vermont, you will probably chance on a country auction. Men are carrying beds and bureaus out of a house, every door of which is wide open. People sit in folding chairs, and the auctioneer holds up a butter churn or sways a Boston rocker.

There are imitations of the true country auction, rummage sales really, run for the benefit of lodge or church. These sales are posted as "The Lord's Auction," and they are often picturesque, taking place on a village green or under the maples at the house of a church deacon whose barns have sheltered the donated articles.

The true auction is not a community or church project. It is the culmination of a family tragedy. A farmer gnarled as his hillside apple trees gives up the battle with land whose only certain crop is stones. A widower lonely as the old man in Theodore Dreiser's story forever seeking his lost Phoebe, who has cooked his solitary messes of bacon and beans on the wood stove, can no longer chop his kindling or stoke his fire. A widow or a maiden lady, the last of a long line, has quietly faded away.

When crippling age narrows activity the public auction is the last event in a sale that has continued for years. First to go are the herds. Three years ago we were saddened by the sight of our neighbor's Alderneys riding away. The drifting progress of these cows up the mountain slopes in morning and back to the barn in late afternoon was as pleasant to watch as the shadows on the hills. For another year our neighbor drove his horses about the mowings, and they too were sold. I stood with another old friend as they rode by, their ears twitching. He looked somberly into the distance and said, "I kept my team as long as I could. We'd done a lot of work together. When I had to let them go I felt mighty bad. The day I took down the harness for the last time I couldn't keep the water out of my eyes. Yes, I felt mighty bad."

After the cattle and horses are

gone, there is a continuous private sale. Men stand in the barnyard reposeful, unhurried. They are buying a grindstone, a saw, a snath, a piece of harness, some tool of a kind made long ago and still familiar to the hand.

Our neighbors were diversified farmers, but when great dairy herds are sold it is not a matter of a few cows led by the halter to adjoining farms. Pedigrees are printed in booklets. Dairymen come from distant states to the formal auction, which is called a dispersal, a solemn word recalling Roman harassment of the Jews.

Most country auctions take place in summer or early autumn when weather and roads are likely to be good. Notices appear in the local papers on Thursday. The sale, unless expected to run more than a day, is usually held on Saturday.

If several auctions are posted, you should choose one on an obscure road of the kind shown only on the maps of The United States Geodetic Survey. You follow brooks. You plunge into lanes bordered by thickets and are sure the rocky crown of the road will scrape out the mechanism of your car, gutting it like a fish. You climb hills at a forty-five degree angle. At last you come out in a clearing. At the foot of high pastures, with a view of valleys to the front and a mountain brook plashing over boulders, you glimpse the weather-beaten buildings and leaning sheds. The auctioneer's boy is setting up chairs in the yard. Salt-corroded cars and trucks of neighbors stand along the lane and at the edge of the mowing, while more fashionable models belong to summer folk who have come to be entertained or to "pick up antiques." Fine antiques still come out of houses like this.

It is an "open and shut day" with cloud shadows dappling the hills. The nephew, executor of the estate, is an old man himself. He sits apart with his wife and daughters, his hands folded on the head of his cane. He watches as the auctioneer's assistants carry out the furniture. If he has childhood associations with the kitchen table or the crockery cookie jar he does not reveal them. He looks beyond the maples to the backdrop of abandoned pasture and mowing sown with rocks that lie on the ledges like sheep among the clumps of juniper.

The harsh daylight reveals mars and patches. The cookstove lacks a leg and is shored up with stones. The paint on the jelly safe is chipped, and the wallpaper with which it is lined, — a pattern of birds in cages, the cages hung among flowering vines — is torn and stained. Six pretty chairs with ash spindles have broken canes. A pile of bed pillows covered with brown and white ticking lost their buoyancy long ago.

The doors of the house are open

Country Auction
M. Colgate

and people wander through, stepping aside when a mattress or commode is carried down the stairs. A pile of fancy work, yellow along the folds, is heaped in a chair. Everywhere is a litter of dust, small dropped articles, bits of paper. A pine chest stands with its drawers open. The contents are tumbled, — a nightgown, crocheted cotton gloves, strings of beads, fragments of lace, a sheet of Christmas wrapping paper, a bit of ribbon, letters tied with a blue bow, leather hair curlers, a skein of embroidery silk, — all the little things a woman saves, hardly knowing why. A gaunt woman, her purse clasped against her chest, looks at the drawers intently as though she were searching for some one thing. She has the expression of asperity that comes of being too long isolated, of knitting dark tangles in the solitary mind. It is hard to know

whether she is thinking, "I too will come to this," or "Nellie had no cause to hold herself so high and mighty." Where low-legged chests and heavy wardrobes have been removed there are mouse nests, and she peers, taking note. On the walls, high up by the ceiling, hang the ancestors, men with billy-goat beards or muttonchop whiskers. They are carried off to be sold for their oval walnut frames.

The auctioneer has begun to "cry" in the yard. His table is set up, and nearby sits the clerk to enter names and prices of goods as they are bid in.

The natives are impassive, enigmatic. They stand or sit with arms folded. Now and then one strolls over to examine something. The strong lines of character show on their faces, and in comparison the summer folk look as alike as so many polished spoons. A young farmer hands his child to his wife and walks to the rack of guns. He takes a rifle, breaks it open, peers down the barrel, looks up the muzzle, tests the sight.

The auctioneer is a favorite among those who practice the trade here. There are schools for auctioneers, and their advertisements appear in agricultural journals. Whether or not this auctioneer attended school, he knows his trade. Licensed by the state to "cry," he is legally bound by certain legislation. He is not per-

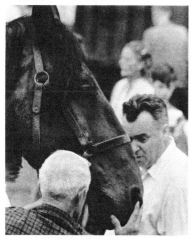
As the livestock go

mitted a claque to fan the bidding. I saw this same auctioneer on a different occasion stop in the midst of lively bidding when a bid came from the woman in whose behalf the auction was held. He explained that certain articles in a certain part of the yard were not hers, but had been brought by him from a warehouse. She was trying to bid up her own goods. A sharp downstroke of the hand closes the sale. No one may edge up afterward and get that Staffordshire plate for ten cents more.

The auctioneer is looking over his audience. A Paisley shawl, a kerosene lamp, a stack of plates are on the table before him. He shakes out the shawl and reports three moth holes. He knows about the current fashion for making jackets of Paisley shawls. He turns the plates and reads the potters' marks. He knows the value of the old copper pots; he is an antiquarian of the first order. He has a singsong like the tobacco auctioneer's. "Two-and-a-half-who'll-pay-two-seventy-five-two-seventy-five-who'll pay." He stops. He changes his pace. He has a ready wit and a sense of humor like Dogberry's. He holds up two soapstone bed warmers. "Fine for bachelors!" An old chamber pot, especially one with a crocheted cozy for the lid or a picture in the bottom, gives him a real opportunity.

He has the comprehensive vision of a fly, aware of movement before, beside, behind him. The stoicism of the crowd is partly self-protection. Slapping at a small mountain fly, lifting a wrist to read a watch, smoothing a lock of hair, even showing excess animation is risky. You can find yourself in the position of Doctor Syntax, who bid up his own book.

AUCTIONEER — "The Book's knocked down at two pound two, The money to be paid by you."

SYNTAX — "This sure is reas'ning most absurd. Why, Sir, I never spoke a word; I might have nodded twice or thrice, To see the book fetch such a price."

AUCTIONEER — "Nodding is bidding, Sir, well known in ev'ry auction-room in town, And now the Book, Sir, is your own."

The Paisley shawls, soapstones, copper pots, old china, glass lamp shades, and such items interesting to collectors go mainly to summer folk. Lodge owners are looking for cheap

11

bedding and chairs. The lumpy pillows sell to a young lodge keeper who
remarks dryly as he carries them off,
"In this business a pillow's a pillow."

The auctioneer now comes to articles of no value to the knowing.
There is a broken set of plain dishes.
A deacon's wife, a stately woman
with gray hair combed smoothly
back buys them and goes forward to
fetch them with a market basket.
A "foreigner" whispers audibly, "I
could do better than that at the dime
store." She smiles, unperturbed. She
knows the prices in the sales order
catalog. She bought the dishes for
the church kitchen and for the sake
of her neighbor, the old man sitting
with his hands on his cane. When
she serves the meatloaf and slaw on
these plates at the next church supper she will know they were Nellie's,
and so will the other women. They
may even break through their reserve
and speak of her.

Auctions are social occasions where
folks meet folks "from over the
mountain," but there is more to it
than that. Attendance is an act of
homage. You go for remembrance's
sake and because neighbors feel responsible for one another. There is
not enough loose cash in Vermont
for people to have formed the city
habit of idle and restless buying. It is
left to summer folk to run up prices
on spindle-legged towel racks and
stone cream jugs; I have been at auctions where weather-beaten farmers
pulled out buckskin pouches and
laid down amazing sums for very
commonplace things: a wooden tub,
zinc sap bucket covers, rakes, saws,
and guns. It was not ignorance that
made them purchase these things.
This is the sort of thing Vermonters
have money for, to stand by an old
neighbor who has fallen on hard
times.

I once went to an auction where
the house was new, as things are
counted new up here. The people
were new. It was not a forced sale,
being a matter of convenience rather

Concentrating on the auctioneer

than of necessity. Grand Rapids furniture went for a handful of silver. The auctioneer was distraught. "Where is the money today! Money is certainly tight today! Where is it?" It would not have been tight if this had been a distress sale and the tables, hooked rugs and china cups had been made valuable by memories of quiet meetings and inarticulate friendships.

The morning passes and shadows shorten. A coffee urn is set up on a trestle table. Sandwiches and cupcakes are laid out on spread paper napkins. The mountain woman who stood contemplating the mouse nests opens a sandwich as one lifts a pot lid and looks inside.

"Hmpf. Short on the fillin! Kingsberry church allus did spread their fillin's mighty thin." She puts cream in her coffee and adds, "Coffee's weak, too. Usin' the grounds twice, I expect." The faces of the women behind the urn are a little red.

Our auctioneer, having got through much kitchen rummage, has come to garments. He opens a carton. "Oh. Hats." He claps one on his head. It is of the layer cake style favored by Queen Mary. The comical effect yet evokes a vision of an austere, gaunt woman with small head and scanty hair, standing with a black umbrella held by both hands like a shepherd's crook. There is a guffaw. An arty summer lady who puts on theatricals buys the whole batch for fifty cents.

No one has been offended by the clowning, which has not changed the tone of underlying solemnity. These people could understand the grave scene in Hamlet, which has puzzled some who live in the sheltered halls of academe. Those who face tragedy totally can laugh without guilt.

Think how reserved the people of northern New England are, and then consider the total exposure involved in a public auction, not the exposure of the final crisis only, but of every little makeshift and dodge — the broken rung on the chair, the holes in the carpet, the handleless cup, the patched blanket, all the attrition of the long retreat into debility and dependence. The anguish of this exposure would be insupportable if it were not for these people's capacity

13

Watching the sale of a
lifetime's accumulation

to accept tragedy. They meet it
shoulder to shoulder, as in a phal-
anx. They face it in all its starkness,
drinking the bitter cup stoically,
without wry expression. It is a matter of principle. It is part of their
Calvinistic heritage, like the grim-
ness of their funerals.

A succession of young seminarians
with new psychological theories
about traumatic experiences, pastors
in the church in our village, have
fought in vain to eliminate the open
coffin at funerals. Man, woman, and
child must march past and behold
the end of man, in the spirit of the
New England Primer, out of which
babes memorized,

Our days begin with trouble
here,

Our life is but a span;
And cruel Death is always near,
So frail a thing is man.

These cautious and laconic people
never commit themselves in answer
to a direct question, but say, "M'ght
be," or, dubiously, "Ayeh." Yet their
papers publish dry and factual sum-
maries of the cases on the docket at
the courthouse in Newfane, whether
the action be civil, divorce, or crimi-
nal. There is no flavor of the scandal
sheet, but neither is there any covering up or any extenuation. All
names are given in an impartial exposure which treats alike the influential and the obscure. One's mind goes
back to the days of Samuel Sewall,
when stern ministers listed on Sabbath the past week's faults and fall-
ings-off of the congregations. This
paradox of cautious reserve and public exposure is startling to one used
to suburban newspapers, which cater
to the suburbanite's image of himself as a successful inhabitant of the
advertiser's paradise.

The exposure is the stark logic
of doomsday. When that trumpet
sounds everything will be told from
the housetops. It follows that if you
steal someone's purse or spread the
fillin' mighty thin, you should be
given a public reprimand.

But when your trouble comes of
the nature of life itself, there can be
solace in what Oscar Wilde called
the "honorable sorrows." Death that
shatters a family, a changing econ-

Counting out the price

right effort, old age, all these are honorable sorrows. The people of New England take them without shame, in silent dignity, as they have taken the wind and the snow and the granite hills.

Country auctions, after one is a long sojourner here, cease to be opportunities to pick up an antique. They are a kind of ceremony which includes the tragic and the comic and which you attend in order to stand with your neighbors in deference to those who are "sold out." If a familiar chair turns up, a chair in which you sat many an hour while your old friend told of her girlhood, ah, that is different. You pull out your not-too-fat purse and lay down a surprising sum.

omy that makes a hill farm submarginal, poverty in spite of noble up-

RASPBERRY CREAM

"Take a quart of thick sweet cream, and boil it two or three wallops; then put it off the fire, and strain the juice of rasberries into it to your taste; stir it a good while before you put your juice in, that it may be almost cold when you mix it, and afterwards stir it one way for almost a quarter of an hour; then sweeten it to your taste, and when cold you may send it up."

Susannah Carter, *The Frugal Housewife* . . . (London, n.d.) , pp. 148-49.

The Way Winter Was

by C. William Chilman

In our Hancock County part of Maine, winter began as a downhill slide, an abrupt taking over, from fall. There is always a merging and a shading together of seasons. But with winter, the onset was so much more incisive, so headlong. Perhaps this was because we dreaded it so, were alert to its imminence, and knew well the long tunnel-winding of its night. Or perhaps, knowing the inexorability of its coming, we were relieved to get on with it and glad, perversely, for whatever joys it could offer.

Always the first snow—like an ambush—struck utterly by surprise. Nothing made ready for it, or bade it welcome. Here still were October's spikes and trailings of grass; here was old goldenrod, the blossoms fluffed and defenseless with age; yonder were oak leaves, windworn and browned now, but still hardy. And the last shrivelled apples clung in the orchard, too small and spotty for gleaning, but not yet devoured by crows. It all seemed too soon, too ahead of itself, too eager to begin.

We met it with a mix of feeling, a shocked but stoic ambivalence. There was first a regret for the leaf and blossom now surely past, the vanished delights of long summer evenings, and the blessed coatlessness of warmth. Then there was pause, as we contemplated the drawnout sadness of short-growing days, the hip-deep struggles through unplowed drifts, the dragging months of freezings and thawings. And with all this, joy—a bounding, buoyant happiness as one shifted gears to the glass-hard perfection of the skating place, the wind-whistle rush of the ski trail, the clean compactness of snowballs, the surfeits of Thanksgiving and splendors of Christmas.

The browns of October had scarcely a chance to deploy themselves. Their time was so brief—the stout russets of oak, the tans of beech, the saffrons of elm, the ancient grasses like litterings of barbered hair. Always caught unawares, these remnants of a season gone were engulfed and soon borne earthward. The leaf-drifts and weed clumps might withstand the first several snows, and the pasture-tussocks might still hold their heads aloft. But inevitably, all were flattened and tamped into place by each succeeding storm. By early December, their downfall was fin-

"Always the first snow struck utterly by surprise."

ished—all but the mouse-runs where weeds had grown thickest, all but the rabbit warrens in the most sheltered briar-pockets.

The marvel was that even in the midst of this sliding together of seasons—the dying of autumn and the advent of winter—were the portents and promises of another spring. In the depths of pasture grass, right against the earth, were sleeping shoots of green. In the naked apple trees, the dormant buds—plainly visible—bode their time and their growing against the cold. Even the twig-ends of spruce, new as of last spring, bore a look of muted vitality. They seemed to secrete within themselves the promissory note of pliant green sprouts to come—moribund now, but surely en route.

The first snow came silently, windlessly. It fell slightly slantwise, from out of a macadam-gray pall. A bone-chilling void of damp awaited it and reached up toward it. Sometimes it spat thickly, with a rustling and a whispering of tiny granules against the cold-stiffness of leaves. There was a hollowness to this, the leaves being rounded and curled with age. Beneath the dense needle-roof of the spruces, the grains sifted themselves to an almost flour-like lightness, dusting the earth around the tree-roots like the dipping of doughnuts in fine sugar.

It gathered in frills and flurries around the edges of things—pasture fringes, walks, flower beds, lawn borders, cart-tracks, pathways, tree bases—then ever so gradually inched its way outward, mantling everything. And all the while, it caught and thickened in the clefts of trees, at the junctures of limbs and trunks, in the corners of steps and the valleys of roofs. It filled the low-lying depressions, the cups and hollows of fields. It clung to the brickwork of chimney tops, dispersed itself in the louvers of window blinds, and put caps on the fenceposts. It frosted the brook banks right down to the water. It hung embroidery on the bare bones of shrubs. It gave decent burial to the fallen banners of autumn. It came misty and soft sometimes, too—kindly-seeming and wearing sheep's clothing.

You could look up into it and see it come. It seemed to materialize—full-blown—out of the grayness twenty feet above your head, and to spring downward in a shower of pint-sized arrows. It hissed past your face, swished against your coat collar, gathered in your sleeve wrinkles. And always it seemed to be breathing, muttering in half-heard sibilants, striving to communicate in loose-lipped syllables. Its sound was like gossip from behind a hand, the words filtered and indistinct, the contents blurred and vaguely suspect.

The earth, drawing warmth from some deep-down hoard, at first appeared to melt this new snow. There was a dampening, a slight semi-wetness, on the surface. It was as if some lingering shred of summer, in a last deathbed rally, half rose in feeble and final protest. But, its breath-warmth soon exhausted, it fell back and gave over. The melting, if any, was illusory and the ground soon folded itself in and hid from view.

Once this happened, it stayed hidden. Except for the bed of a well shovelled path, the slope of a stream bank exposed to the sun, or a road shoulder abraded by a passing plow, the earth didn't show its face again until late March. The first snows appeared to shrink, even recede, a little. But like the illusion of melting, this was soon done. They were speedily renewed. From late November on, snow could fall daily—in heavy, wide-apart flake clusters that drifted dreamily down, in sudden

"The rains and brook-burstings of April were a long, uphill distance away." *Photo by James C. Ward.*

squalls and blusters, in grainy plummetings that stung your face, in swirling blizzards that blew up your nostrils and set them tingling, and in finely drawn sprinklings that slipperied the ice and draped the spruces with filmy new clothing. Each new layer settled upon the one beneath, shaking itself down like a hen in her dust bath. Always the mass became more compact—thickening and heavying itself as the weeks passed. By sheer dint of its own weight and volume, it pressed an ice sheath over the earth, tough as bedrock. It locked the earth in, turned the key, then threw this key away.

There were two faces of winter, I felt. The beautiful face was the rarer, like a lovely woman appearing fleetingly at an open casement. This was the face of a sub-zero

"Each new layer settled upon the one beneath." *Photo by James C. Ward.*

brilliance, a cobalt-blue early morning after a night-long cascade fall of powder. Skis were invented for moments like this. Bone dry, waxed, and rubbed to a dance floor slipperiness, they flew by themselves. To get out early was the thing, before the sun generated a whisper of warmth, before trackings disturbed the surface, and before winds toppled the snow freight from the branches. There was so little time, this fragile loveliness was so brief, the perfection was so exquisite, that one's perceptions boggled. They could not be mobilized quickly enough or focus narrowly enough to grasp details, but instead became tangled in generalized wonderment. Unscrambling them, finally, one first felt the silence. It had to be felt, for it was the total hush of engulfment, of muffled standstill. It was everywhere —in the half-light calm of the spruce woods, in the ice-blue shadows of pasture corners, in the sunlit be-

dazzlement of clearings and back lanes. There was an expectant, waiting quality about it, too, as if all life and activity were in suspension, until this blinding and blanketing should pass. Not even a crow caw or a squirrel scold could be heard.

And then one's awareness took in the spruces and fir balsams, especially the youthful, more svelte ones that stood apart or in small, choosy groups. Loaded with ermine cappings of new powder, their branches down-drooped, slope-shouldered, like fur-coated women in wide Dolman sleeves.

The snow crystals at this hour were jewel-perfect. They lay loose and free, like weightless wisps of congealed sunbeams. No sun warmth had settled them, no breeze had yet breathed away their angles and frost points. Million upon cold million they lay, glittering diamond-hard in the reflected hauteur of the sun. And save for a now-and-then rabbit lollop or the skitter track of a mouse, all lay as they had fallen, undefiled and still.

Silver birches arched to the ground were another of winter's beauties. Two or three times a year, a freezing drench of rain would sheathe everything—even the last upright spindle of old grass—in a murderous glaze of ice. The birches doubled right over then, bowed like willow withes to their nethermost twig ends. Only as a half-thaw loosened the grip of the ice did they right themselves, stiffly and gradually, like old men rising from low chairs.

Yet another loveliness was the window frost of a zero morning. This fillip of winter required no bundling against the outside cold, for there it was, right in the room with you. Always, each pane was its own unique contrivance of pattern—masses of jungle fern here, banana foliage and acanthus engravings here, comet swirls and Spanish bayonets yonder. Sometimes there were blank areas of glistening frost like bits of sky, vistas of water, or open meadows. But each tracery caught the sun glint differently, and each was its own illusion of shading and sparkle.

The other face of winter was housemaid dull and plain. It was the face of dreary sameness, of endless indistinction. It was the back side of the Christmas card. It was the craggy unyielding of frozen slush, the nameless footprints petrified in ice ce-

ment. It was the stove ashes, poured on slippery paths, that stuck to your boots. It was the great crinkled icicles that dragged from the eaves like fangs. It was the day-in-day-out thwacking of tire chains out on the main road. It was bitter northwest wind scouring the snow surface in serrated whorls and cutting off your breath with its violence. And it was the frozen pastel of gray-pink dawns, the steam of salt water in Frenchman's Bay, the searching fingers of night cold under a door.

Just as winter had these separate faces, it also had two time spans. The first, really a continued dying of autumn, was a slow-motion tailspin that ended with New Year's. The ever shortening days, the deepening snow, the growing pang of cold, all abetted this illusion of downspiralling. Thanksgiving and Christmas were the milestones of this downhill, darkening time. Once past the shortest day, once over the tinselly spasm of the holidays, once confronted with ever so slightly greater daylight, we felt a corner had been turned.

This was not a sharp corner to be rounded abruptly at a tight angle. It was more a wide, outflowing curve. The added minutes of sunlight were as yet imperceptible, the thermometer continued to plunge, and the bitter plain of January had yet to be crossed.

But one felt the floor of the valley

"This fragile loveliness was so brief."
Photo by Katherine Knowles.

had been gained, that the descent into the trough had evened out. This was a new year, a rebirth of resolution, a renouncing of the decay and error of old year gone. Looking forward, dreaming a little, were possible now, where two months ago, back in early November, they would not have been. Now was the time of seed catalogues, livid with Paul Scarlett roses, magnificently alive with long-podded green peas, absolutely galvanizing with magenta zinnias. Like holy pictures, these catalogues were symbols of faith, of ultimate rebirth, of hope on the way to renewal.

And now was the time for the prognosticators to speculate, restively, on the duration of winter. Though no Maine groundhog had ever been silly enough to expose himself—weak-kneed and half-conscious—to the Candlemas chill of February, the old myth persisted. "Will he *see* his shadow?" queried the wonderers solemnly. "Will there *be* six more weeks of winter?" all the while knowing full well that whatever he did or failed to do, two more months was the uttermost, hardscrabble minimum. Was the hog spleen swollen or lean, they asked. Did the worker bees, last early fall, store their honey high up in trees, or below ground? Were the brown-black caterpillars unusually shaggy or was their fuzz just so-so? When the Farmer's Almanac, in play-it-safe generics, predicted squalls and blizzards for northern New England in late February, did it refer to the coast or the inland regions?

All this meant was a wishfulness, an almost prayerful ploy of fantasy that *this* winter, of all remembered or legendary winters, would be different. Always there was this mindless yearning for surcease, for some quirk of jet stream winds, ocean currents, or even divine indulgence that would shave winter's tedium by a week, two weeks, even three. But in the candor kernel of his consciousness, everyone knew this couldn't happen. There was no help for it— the rains and brook-burstings of April were a long, uphill distance away, a slow climb out of the valley. You coped, you endured, you put up with it. And sometimes there really

21

was a lull-thaw in late January, and a certain openness, or sparseness, of snowfall.

Mixed in with all this and shooting it through like a sunbeam was the fun side of winter. That was the marvel of it, that it could be so joy-packed, so absolutely happiness-making. There was the crust that formed with a freezing rain. You could slide, at your thrilling peril, twice as far, twice as fast, at a whizzing, wind-singing clip. Or you could, if still pre-adolescent and under no pressure to prove yourself, careen wildly down hillsides in dishpans or trays. Or you could carve out a tombstone from the surface crust, print your own epitaph, dig your own grave and lie in it, gazing skyward and knowing exactly how it felt to be "dead."

Wettish snow ("packing" snow, we called it) opened up other delights, snowballs among them. One was snow castles, miniature, many-roomed, many-levelled affairs that were patted and shaped by hand, with domed roofs, snowball steeples, and pillared porches, the columns molded with a jelly glass. The trick with these was to coax the cat inside, block up the doorway, then have her pip her way out, like a chick from its shell. And there were snow forts, great masses of piled up balls with the chinks filled in. One began with a hand-size snowball, rolled it along the surface while it gathered and grew hugely, then shoved or lifted it in place. A variation was a four-sided fort with a door and branches laid across the top as roof supports. And if you really got carried away, you could add outside stairs, lookouts, and parapets, then hope for a freeze.

And of course the ice, skating ice, cloudy gray-black, slick and even as glass. Even the dullest and loosest clamp skate could twinkle over it in effortless skims and flashes. A brook was the thing, a straightaway, pasture-type brook uncluttered by fences or rocks. Only an off wind could stand in one's way, that and old poke-ups of grass at the edges.

In certain extremes of weather, a pasture brook like this could flood, wash over a wide surface, then freeze in successive layers as the waters receded. These ice sheets, one below the other, were wafer-thin, some frosted on one side and smooth on the other, some swirled and marble-ized-wavy, others fern-leaved and frost-flowered. It was wonderfully aggression-releasing to pick up great sheets of this glaze-fine stuff and dash it against the thicker, more rugged ice. There it would shatter in a thousand tinkling splinters, like hated windows one longed to smash but couldn't.

One forgets, in absentia or out of season, how multiformed snow can be. One always remembers it as virginal, crystalline-perfect, and feathery, as it first falls in November. One forgets the slush-ooze, dark with dirt. One banishes from memory the sting of wind-driven granules, fine as talcum. One never recalls the rottenness of March, the melt-freeze graininess of old snowbanks. One disremembers the crust beneath evergreens, pocked with bark fragments and ancient needles. But, ah, why should not one forget what resists savory remembrance? So much that was good was born of the snow; the exquisite lacework of twigs newly dusted, the delicate tracery of frosted fence wire, the inside firmness of a drift, fine as old marble.

That was the thing about winter, this mix of ambivalence, this carnival of this-way and that-way feeling. No other season called up such an intertwined excess of moodiness, foreboding, and pure joy. Man, woman, and beast were humbled by it, tamed by it, made aware of their dependence on one another, and their utter inability to cope alone and unaided. This was a deep-down knowledge, an almost instinctive thing. And this knowing that one had alliance with others was what made it all possible. It lightened the drudging and shored up the spirit. It eased winter's drag and made manifest its beauty.

One late January morning dawned absolutely hushed and motionless. There was sun, yes, but like sub-Arctic moonlight, pale-faced and without warmth. There was a faint bluish coloration in the packed sheathing of snow, in the white clapboarding of houses, in the nakedness of trees, even in the air itself. It was the inner blue one sees in overhangs of very thick and very cold ice. The plumes of early smoke from neighbors' chimneys rose straight up, cottony and pale pink-blue, like vapor trails in the vacuum of outer space. But outside, after breakfast, it didn't seem unusually cold—at first. Then you noticed that with each indrawn breath, your nostrils crinkled and stung, as though being sucked down inside. And that your cheeks and the outer edges of your ears stiffened and quickly turned numb. And that mouth breathing was like swallowing a hot dagger. You sensed, too, the utter stillness.

After ten minutes, you beat a retreat to the kitchen. Having thawed a massive layer of frost from one of the window panes, Father now said, "come here and look at the glass." He always called our big outside window thermometer "the glass." At first glance, the mercury seemed to have shrunk totally from sight. Then you saw it far down, farther down than you had ever dreamed possible. "The glass" read 47 below!

Winter was a continuum of wet socks. It was boot-wet on the floor. It was the gray-on-gray of leaden sky through the rib cages of trees. It was an endlessness of fire stoking, animal tending, and nose running. It was the limb-gnashing roar of wind. It was being fresh out of sugar, with the store a mile away. It was the back break and heart knocking of drive shovelling. It was cranking the Ford and pouring hot water over the engine. It was longjohn underwear on the clothesline, frozen stiff. And it was silence, and aloneness.

But just as much so, it was the gladsome shout from the skating place that quickened one's running so as not to miss a minute of it. It was the delicious slipperiness of a bobsled track in a country road. It was the folds and secret places under snowladen juniper. It was the blue-purple shadowings of a moonlit midnight, with snow squeaking underfoot. It was homecoming to kitchen warmth and supper smells at freezing twilight. It was lamplight streaming from a familiar window, bathing the snow in wide-angle radiance. And most of all, it was safety and shelter and love.

HURRICANES ARE NOTHING NEW

"They [Mr. & Mrs. Freeman of Cambridgeport, Massachusetts] on their journey past & saw the spot where lately stood the house & barns [Smith's Tavern in Orange, Mass.] now swept clear of every movable they had by the wind Sabbath eve before last & scattered for many many miles. One of the feather beds was found on Hubbardston common, and many boards, shingles &c were found in this Town, supposed to come from Orange — a heavy drag & chain was found looped on a tree — about half of the roof of a barn was found in Fitzburg supposed to come from that quarter or region — the family (Mr. Smiths) saved their lives probably by going into the celler, except a girl, who was crushed to death by the tavern — Two houses in Northfield were blown down — and twelve barns were swept away in the course of the hurricane. Four lives were lost & several people wounded — How grateful ought we to be who escaped this awful scene."

MS Journal of Ruth Henshaw Bascom, 17 Sept. 1821. American Antiquarian Society.

The Cold Summer of 1816 in Vermont

FACT AND FOLKLORE

by T. D. Seymour Bassett

"The summer of 1816—ten inches of snow in June, when people froze to death in the month of roses—suicides through fear that the sun was cooling off," recalled nonagenarian James Winchester of Vermont, who was fourteen at the time.

The snowstorm of June 17 broke about noon, and my uncle started for the sheep pasture a mile through the woods, to fix a shelter for the sheep. As he went out the door he told my aunt, "If I'm not back in an hour, call the neighbors and come after me. June is a bad month to be buried in the snow, especially so near July!"

Night fell, bitter cold, and the road was near impassable with drifts. My aunt sent me and my twelve-year-old cousin to the neighbor's a mile away, and we barely got through. Others were roused, and searched the woods until morning. They found the sheep huddled under a shelter of boughs, and on the third day of the search, my uncle, frozen stiff, buried in the snow, a mile in the opposite direction from home.

All summer the wind blew fierce and cold from the north, with very little rain. July was colder than June, and August colder than July. Farmers wore heavy overcoats and mittens about their work every day. James Gooding killed all his cattle and then hung himself. No firewood accumulated for winter: it was needed in the summer. There was not a green thing to be seen.

This excerpt from the Concord, New Hampshire, *Monitor* of the 1890's is typical of the stories handed down or written in local histories about "the Famine Year," "the Scarce Year," "the Poverty Year," "the Year without a Summer," "Eighteen Hundred and Froze to Death." The embroidery varies. Some say that the sheep had just been sheared, and they saved some by tying the fleeces back around their bodies.

Every farmer in Dorset, Vermont, faced with little fodder to winter the stock, brought his sheep to Pea Street, Anna Gilbert's father told her. By that brook they slaughtered thousands. They divided up the wool, hides, tallow, and as much mutton as they could salt or put on ice. A few sheep squeaked through the winter on browse.

Others say the beeches did not put out their leaves again that year; the people survived on boiled nettles, clover heads, wild turnips, and hedgehogs. They walked miles to swap potash for flour and seed corn.

Down in Walpole, New Hampshire, they say Thomas Bellows had a bumper crop on his Connecticut River intervale farm. To men who had lost their crops in the North Country he sold small amounts at low prices and let them work it out if they had nothing to barter. But a speculator trying to buy up what he had left in order to make a killing was turned away.

Elsie Wells, Bakersfield historian, tells why School District Number Ten in the northeast corner of town is still called Egypt. Nathaniel Foster saved his cornfield by cutting and burning pines day and night around the edge, and had enough seed corn for his neighbors from "Canaan."

There is a grain of basic truth, and more, in all this folklore. Vermonters, brought up on it, know that Vermont has two seasons—winter and the Fourth of July. But they have picked violets in December and parked their skis during a January thaw. Could it really have been that cold in the *summer* of 1816?

The facts were so well known at the time that few people bothered to put them down. A few volunteer weathermen with thermometers, and a few editors and diarists have recorded enough to piece together the true story.

The winter of 1815–16 was mild, especially February, but there were several late snows and a backward, dry spring, until the memorable cold wave of June 6–11. Wednesday, June 5, was hot and sultry, with heat lightning. A cold front crossed Lake Champlain after dawn on Thursday and reached the Connecticut River before noon. The temperature dropped forty to fifty degrees and farmers woke to a cold rain, gradually turning to snow and melting as it hit the ground. It whitened Moosilauke, Ascutney, and Killington peaks. The next day stayed cold; travelers could not cross the Lake at Chimney Point into the violent west wind. On Saturday, much more snow: eighteen inches in Cabot, a foot near Randolph, six inches near Rutland, three in Chester, and none south of the Massachusetts line. Frost on Sunday was in many places the most severe.

It was not a local storm. From western New York, Ohio, and as far as the frontier came reports of the same freeze. No one was ready. People donned winter clothes and watched the blackened fields and gardens or gathered in dismay around fires.

Nor was the deepening gloom of the following weeks localized. Editors pasted foreboding news from Quebec, Poughkeepsie, Canandaigua, Kentucky, West Jersey, and Virginia; a thunder-gust at Northampton June 23rd; a July hailstorm in Bradford County, Pa.; an August earthquake in Aberdeen, Scotland; floods on the Rhine. Heavy, cold rains ruined crops from Sweden to Italy. An October fire in Oxford County, Maine, raced through the tinder-dry forests up the Androscoggin from Paris to Bethel. Millers closed for repairs without mentioning their short supply of grain and their trickle of water.

The cold facts behind these observations were reported to the journals by college professors checking their thermometers daily at 7 a.m. and 2 and 9 p.m. It *was* the coldest summer in the history of the Republic, five degrees colder than usual. July and August averaged about 65°, only a little better than June, and the rains were late and light. Even down in Virginia, Thomas Jefferson recorded under six inches of rain at Monticello, instead of the usual fourteen, and an average temperature two to four degrees lower in June and July. The whole world, in fact, was more than a degree and a half below normal that year, as far as existing weather stations could tell, and 1817 was colder.

The crops *were* poor. Light frosts about July 8 and in middle and late August in some places killed most of the corn, some of the large insurance crop of potatoes, and the other Indian vegetables—cucumbers, squash, and beans. "Indian corn," said the Concord *New Hampshire Patriot*, "on which a large proportion of the poor depend, is cut off." "The worst crop known in the his-tory of man," mourned a Weare, New Hampshire, diarist. Caleb Hendee's Pittsford, Vermont, diary recorded no haying until July 22; he did not finish until August 30. The other grains, however, did pretty well, and fruits were often heavy on the branch.

We also know the crops were poor because of the high prices listed in the New York and Boston newspapers and from farm accounts. Some of the lucky and foresighted were charging what the traffic would bear. Shakers in the Berkshires, "influenced by a pretended prophetess," said one account, began the first of August to hoard for a seven-year dearth. The broad Champlain Valley, warmed by the Lake, escaped the frost; so did western New York, warmed by the broader Lake Ontario.

The Northeast Kingdom, latest settled towns near the Canadian border, had none of the fat of good years stored to compensate the lean, and was hit hard. In some towns like Worcester and Navy (now Charleston) a general flight southward took place. Perhaps those hippies of 1817, noticed in local histories as followers of Isaac Bullard and calling themselves Pilgrims, were just some poor, superstitious, transient, starveling ex-settlers from the Eastern Townships of Quebec.

Nobody froze to death, not that summer. "The man who froze his feet in June last in Peacham is like to recover," reported the Danville *North Star*—nothing worse. This episode may contain the kernel of truth in James Winchester's story. According to Bogart's history of Peacham, James Walker, 82, went to look for sheep June 8, missed his way, spent two nights in the woods, and had to have toes amputated.

Livestock suffered, to be sure— hogs and cattle were slaughtered earlier and in larger numbers than usual, in anticipation of provender shortage. The daily menu featured meat and fish. Beef prices usually peaked in August, declining as the droves came in, but in 1816 drovers were on the move all summer and prices fell to a bottom of under $8 a barrel. Pork, preferred to beef, dipped under $20 sooner. Some sheep, prematurely shorn, did die outside Quebec City, but in Vermont they were not generally washed and clipped until late June. The snow-fed streams were too cold.

The most amazing thing about such amazing weather is that almost nobody wrote much about it at the time. The Bennington *Vermont Gazette* reported the Bennington Battle Day celebration August 16: "It was a delightful day and amid the pressure of an exuberant harvest, farmer and mechanic intermingled in tumultuous joy, hasted from the shop and field to the former rendezvous of the heroes under Stark."

Reports of Fourth of July celebrations mention a Hinesburgh death from a pistol's misfiring, and the usual paeans to Freedom, but not the weather. President Samuel Austin of the University of Vermont was silent too when he opened the legislature with an election day sermon October 10. The governors of New Hampshire, New York, and Vermont, however, in their annual messages and Thanksgiving Day proclamations, did barely mention the diminished harvest, and counseled thrift.

The judgment of God was not a common explanation, although one Hyde Park rhymester entitled his effort, "Rambling stanzas, on the extraordinary cold the past spring &c. A.D. 1816 and fearful apprehensions by many expressed of starving for want of bread; and wild corus [*sic*] of moving to the West & South, to run away from the Judgments of God." Middlebury Congregationalists did appoint June 21 as a day of fasting and prayer, obviously because of the bad season, and the visiting preacher rang the changes on God's punishing the people for their sins. But this was a form, repeated from force of habit.

The dominant note was secular. The typical reaction in the press speculated about natural causes. Did icebergs, volcanic eruptions, or sun spots cause the cold? Dr. Samuel L. Mitchill wrote in the New York *Med-*

ical Repository that some Arctic upheaval had loosed more and larger icebergs into the Atlantic. Popular and influential as ex-Congressman Mitchill was, the common man remembered the steady westerlies, and could not see how they could have blown cold air off the Atlantic. He could see "the spider in the sun" with the naked eye—a series of unusually large and clustered sun spots, which meteorologists still associate with cold spells. Another contemporary theory that has not been discredited is the pollution of the atmosphere with the dust of tremendous volcanic explosions. Intense volcanic activity beginning in 1812 was climaxed in April 1815 by the greatest of known explosions on the island of Sumbawa east of Java. Tamboro, hitherto considered extinct, emitted 37 to 100 *cubic miles* of dust, ashes, and cinders, burying villages forty miles around and killing 60,000. The dust reddened sunsets around the world and, experts say, blocked the sun's radiation, lowering the earth's temperature.

The region recovered from this setback as from the War of 1812, spotted fever, and British trade competition. Samuel Goodrich re-called the stampede from Connecticut after the war, but it did not begin then. As soon as there was a chance to go to warmer climes and richer lands, some Yankees took it. Samuel Crafts, later Congressman and Governor, seriously considered becoming a Mississippi planter in 1802. The postwar depression, glowing reports of " 'tother side of Ohio," the habits of rolling-stone frontiersmen all built up pressures to leave. Few contemporaries suggested this cold summer as a cause, yet the *series* of cold years, 1812–18, contributed toward making people want to leave.

The folklore of that impossible summer provides a handy symbol of the end of an era. The age of making easy money on wild land, or good crops on the humus of newly cleared land, or having the thrill of getting there first, was over for Vermont. The stories said, Vermont is a cool place, but not the El Dorado it was. If you think you can take it when it gets as bad as the summer of 1816, stay. Otherwise start looking for a warmer place. Many started looking, and arranging to sell out and travel, so that in the decade ending in 1820, over 200,000 went West from New England.

What Is This about New England?

by David Cornel DeJong

People have asked me, and I have come to ask it of myself: "What is this about New England that you prefer it over any other region of the country and have chosen to live there, and even find yourself thinking and behaving like a New Englander?"

It isn't too difficult a question to answer, especially in the beginning. You have a new affection, you marvel about it; you have something of a right to be incoherent and impressionistic. Later you plan to come up with a more formal, logical answer, after you have weeded or sorted out opinions and emotions. For the time being you give more or less expected answers.

It is an altogether different matter to answer yourself honestly. Logic is seldom effective because it is too formal and aloof. Emotions are not to be trusted, while integrity is rarely under your own control. The truth may in fact lie wholly outside yourself. But it is you yourself that you are concerned with, and accordingly you have to get to the core of the matter.

My own preconceived notions about New England were largely borrowed from others. I am a foreigner, a Hollander, and the Dutch in me needs particular conviction. For some time before coming to New England I had made it a practice to live in as many representative regions of the United States as my meager finances and circumstances allowed.

By the time I came to New England, to Providence and Rhode Island in particular, I had behind me twelve years of childhood in my native Holland, behind the dikes on the shores of the North Sea, in a fishing village. It was a wonderful boyhood. Then followed several years in the Midwest, being absorbed by or absorbing whatever brand of American culture Michigan has to offer, while learning to express myself in English. Next came a few mixed years of living in the Deep South and in New York. In between I traveled to every state in the Union except one, which I missed by a fluke. Ubiquitously at least I behaved like a convert-American; surely the unequal enthusiasm of converts possessed me.

I set foot in Providence on a Sunday afternoon, after an ogling jour-

ney by train through the width of Massachusetts, during which I embraced enthusiastically everything I saw and encountered, even my first detection of the New England accent. There seemed to be something definite and honest about the region. When I emerged from the Union Station in Providence I found myself in a receptive mood, even though I was encountering a strange city destined to be my home.

Photo courtesy of the Rhode Island Development Council.

I had no misgivings. I was unprepared. I had abandoned any preconceived notions. Yet I found myself saying: "This is it. Here I belong." Even though I realized my reaction amounted to intoxication, for the moment I was allowing my animal senses and my sentiments to take over.

For one thing, I was breathing in sea air. But I had done that elsewhere, and here it was somewhat contaminated by the brackish river. I was watching swooping gulls. Where I had been born and brought up, gulls and terns had swooped over me constantly. But above all, below me lay a crowded and clustered city, and I, coming from a clustered country, had never felt particularly intimate with too spacious and profuse Michigan. There

was much lovely old red brick, gables, walls, turrets . . . Oh, yes, I was submitting myself to poetic license, which in turn is not to be defined nor even paraphrased.

These were first impressions, however, and favorable, no matter how inchoate. They were intimate reactions, to which I added a conscious feeling of affection and kinship, something to be reckoned with in an utterly strange region and city. These feelings prompted me to keep on living in New England no matter what the charms elsewhere. My liking was to fan out from Providence and minuscule Rhode Island to the rest of the region. It would eventually expand from emotions and experiences to a consummate affection and acceptance.

Along the way and through the years I tried to give myself an accounting, although, perhaps subconsciously, I preferred to delay it, because I favored the process of living and experiencing. Accounting, after all, is tantamount to standing still, taking stock and looking back; it calls for readjustment, realignment, and reconsideration. I felt New England was a region and an essence that had to be experienced gradually. I wanted to keep living those experiences and adding to them. New England seemed to be worth it, and already I loved it.

By way of preparation, there were my previous experiences in other

parts of the country. After leaving Holland, I had to push through the difficult, formative years in Michigan, made more unbearable because I had been severely uprooted. My prejudices convinced me that life in the new country, and in Michigan in particular, was full of untoward foibles. There was always a striving toward something larger and further away. I felt that I was forever being asked to push on and look ahead; never mind what lay behind me since it had no value in the American way of life. The past had no dignity, the present no significance. Everything lay in a sort of chaotic future. I had to tie my wagon to that amorphous star called Ambition.

I became, in consequence, too troubled by the fact that I was an alien, my past amiss and baleful, a blot. I allowed myself to think I should deny my birthright, and of course, I lacked the perspective to think otherwise. Nor, on the other hand, did I have the peace of mind that would allow me to be absorbed by the new civilization. I felt that I was being pushed in every possible direction, while still obeying the one great admonition: to catch up, keep up, and deny my alien background.

Next came my few years in the South. There was much I liked about that section of the country, even if much of its life seemed exclusive and diluted. After Michigan, it was at least relaxing. Even so, I gathered there that all things really cogent had already been lived, that it was much more civilized to point back. Accordingly, it was hardly urbane to consider the effort of becoming a well-rounded American as anything worthy of one's best energy.

Of course in the South, too, I was a "foreigner," but with a difference. In North Carolina and Georgia I was a cute foreigner, always adolescent, fair-haired, and sweetly quaint. I was the traditional boy holding a pink finger in the green dike. Before long I felt that it didn't matter how I lived or what I absorbed just as long as I allowed myself to remain the embodiment of a sentiment. I could remain static but beneficent.

Next I lived in New York, where historically and ethnically you aren't really anything; not an entity, neither an alien nor a citizen, neither a forward-marching pilgrim nor a sort of Mr. Lot, doomed to look back only. You are there on suf-

33

Photo courtesy of the M Dept. of Commerce.

ferance. In a way, I liked it. It was a strengthening experience after the Middle West and the South. It was also a lonesome experience. It did not make for love, nor did it add up to reverence for the place I lived in.

I made my much briefer excursions to the forty-odd states outside New England. Then circumstances called me to New England itself. When I came, perhaps biased by living in the South, I was determined I would not be impressed by New England's antiquity nor awed by its traditions and history. Everybody thought I should be, but where I had spent my childhood things had been even older, more intricate, certainly as glorious. Besides, hadn't I learned to be suspicious of the past and the traditions fostered by it?

Something happened, however. In spite of my intentions, I realized almost from the beginning that in New England tradition and history were being lived with; the past was not enshrined, not denied, not glorified, but experienced, together with the all-important present. It was an

eye opener, a mind and soul opener, yet I felt I should not be overimpressed. There had to be a gimmick somewhere, and experience would show it up. In the meanwhile I had better attribute my sudden liking for the region to something simpler.

There was the sea. It provided me with an answer. Yet it wasn't like my Dutch sea which had always been a challenge, an enemy, a presence you could never ignore, nor quite live away from, like an officious parent. The New England sea was more majestic, rock-rimmed, less man-controlled, never really intimate. It was simply a fearful and wonderful entity.

The New England topography. Yes, I could prefer it to the pool-table flatness and greenness of Holland. But rocks and rills do not affection make. And I had seen the rest of the United States. The New England mountains and valleys were lovely and varied; but elsewhere I had seen them larger and more impressive. Further, I knew I could not love nor live for topog-

raphy only. It satisfies for such a short time, unless nostalgia is connected with it. The New England climate? I think it is pretty wonderful and beats that of Holland and Michigan all to pieces, but it isn't enough to sustain one, and mountains, rivers, and coastlines aren't sufficient to shape one.

Pretty soon I ran out of externals as explanations, especially those related to nature. There remained the cities and towns. But many were ugly and cluttered, without plan or pattern, even if others were lovingly intimate and picturesque. On the other hand, towns and cities add up to people. People live in them and are responsible for them. Yet lovely people live in mad beehives of cities and miscreants in the daintiest of villages. Ah yes, but on the whole, and as I rubbed elbows with them, and grinned at them and beyond them, it was the New England people I loved most. More than I had loved people anywhere else, so you couldn't blame my occupational pretenses. As a practising writer it be-

comes part of one's stock in trade to love and understand people, those objective extensions and aberrations of oneself.

Why then did I, do I, love New Englanders? In the first place I did not have to limit myself to liking the old-time Yankees and their current-day equivalents. In the cities at least there was a far greater proportion of resettled Italians, Irish, Portuguese, and Poles, to prevent me from seeing clearly the true native stock. Particularly in the beginning. Yankees are very private people. So I saw the others first, and you couldn't even call them equivalent Yankees.

Or could you? Something had palpably happened to these "foreigners," something had penetrated them. They threw off an aura of assimilation which did not smack of a leveling-off, a kowtowing-to, or a rising-above. They had achieved a pride in privacy and in the individual which I had not found elsewhere. What, then, had happened to them?

I had been warned about New

Photo courtesy of the Connecticut Development Commission.

Photo courtesy of the Mass. Dept. of Commerce.

England hospitality. It was supposed to be something negative; if it existed at all, it would be cold and sparing. Nothing could be further from the truth.

From the beginning I found New Englanders — vintage or relatively new — the friendliest and most genuinely hospitable people I had come across anywhere in the country. The New England brand of hospitality might be a bit austere, say, by Texan standards, but it is invariably dignified and of human stature. One is never crushed by it, and then asked to stand back and answer the fulsome: "Well, how do you like my crushing welcome? Don't it beat everybody and everything?"

Here in New England hospitality seems to be qualified in these terms: "Look, this is what we are, and you are what you happen to be. Let us not embarrass each other by bandying emotions foreign to us. Let us take each other as we are, amenably, and then find out gradually where and on what plane we can best meet. Meanwhile we each have a chance to preserve our dignity, haven't we?"

As I said, newcomers have been leavened by such hospitality. It is not a part and parcel of the rocks and rivers, neither is it exuded by them. Perhaps we should blame the older inhabitants. Still, their attitude is stigmatized as coldness. It is lacking, isn't it, without grace or exhilaration? Possibly. It truly does not lend itself to self-projection. Unlike that of the South, the New England attitude doesn't act like something extracted from a code book or pulled from behind a golden frame and hardly expected to be acted upon, unless of course, you happen to be "one of ours" to start with. It certainly isn't the pre-occupied indifference of New York. New England hospitality is something to be lived; not from a sudden beginning to a sudden end, not from an expansive gesture to an already visible saturation point, but something which becomes a part of life and experience, and for which you are allowed time and opportunity, while you keep breathing and are allowed your own conscience.

In a way, New England hospitality is the essence of old Yankeedom. It has also been earmarked, negatively, as an aspect of Puritanism. It has become indigenous, assimilated by all and sundry who are civil and willing.

Let me approach it from a rather oblique angle. I always felt that New England hospitality, decor, and dignity had something Dutch about them, to which accordingly the Dutch in me reacted. Of course, most Dutch are Calvinists, too. I have a thorough-going Yankee wife, born and bred here. When for the first time I showed her Holland — and on each subsequent return — she would ask: "Why do I feel at home in this country, among its people? Why do I keep being reminded of the natives of Maine and Rhode Island, where I was brought up?" Between us we attempted to sort out our reactions, my initial ones in regard to New England, hers in response to my native country, and in particular to my province of Friesland, which by more than one observer has been tagged the New England of the Netherlands. Furthermore, Dutchmen, and Frisians more specially, are often described as dour, reserved, exclusive, too damned stubborn and independent for comfort.

We tried to figure it out, my wife and I, experience by experience, impression by impression. It wasn't until we returned from our third trip that we arrived at something like an answer. We decided it was the people, the natives. We agreed that it was the people who were genuinely *with* you. Not for you or against you, not ready to embrace you, but they were with you as fellow human beings. You were what you were, an individual, someone private, hence important. In turn they implied that they were too.

I had sensed this privacy in New Englanders for a long time, but I hadn't felt the need to crystalize my feelings. No New Englander, for instance, hands you his emotions on a platter and invites you to make a banquet of them. He would rather, very much cat-like, turn his back and allow you to think what you wish, but requires that you be civilized enough to leave what belongs to him exclusively with him, where it belongs. He doesn't exclude you pointedly; rather, he assumes certain premises. He applies them to grief, for instance, and to love. Both are emotions to be taken indoors and not left to roam at loose, where they may lead to discomfort or excess. Call it aloofness, and it is, but it is an urbane aloofness.

Here I am living in New England and calling myself a New Englander, and I have never been gainsaid by any Yankee. No one finds it necessary to remind me that I am foreign-born. Previously and elsewhere too much condescension, or indifference, or even reverence for the old made me feel apart. Now the question remains: was I merely ready for New England, or is New England there, receptive to all who understand its peculiar dignity? With me both are true, even if from time to time I still find doors closed to me. They should remain closed until a certain interrelationship has become more inclusive.

I keep asserting that New England is a full-bodied experience, a complete one, which involves its past and antiquities as much as its amalgamated present and casually prepared-for future. I find a kinship with its people. Its true essence is exuded by its towns and extended by its cities, but never in evangelistic fashion. And so my reactions remain on the poetic side, but I dare say that any enumeration of anecdotes and details would add little to my basic conclusions.

The Family Dentist

by Mildred McClary Tymeson

Two wars had been fought and won since the Flaggs, the Greenwoods, the Reveres had lived as neighbors in the north end of Boston and together had survived smallpox, kept shops, suffered hard times, and made a country's history.

Now even the town was different. In fact, in this year of 1822, Boston had become a city.

The Stone House on Beacon Street, advertised as such by Josiah Flagg to identify it from the many wooden houses that ran up close to the narrow cobblestone street, was no longer there.

Neither was the hill, at least not as it used to be.

Shovelful by shovelful, the hills of Boston were being leveled. The valleys and ponds were being filled in; the land was nudging the bay farther and farther away. But there was still the sea—the wonderful, bountiful sea, which for so long had linked the town to the rest of the world.

In Boston's Almanac of 1822 the City claimed no more special distinction than that here, under the wide elm arms of its Liberty Tree, had originated the Revolution "which gave Independence to America."

"Neither clergy, lawyers, physicians, nor literary men," said Henry Adams, "were much known beyond the State." In 1800 except for the physician hardly a man in Boston earned his living by science or by art. Emerson went so far as to say that between 1780 and 1820 there was not a book, a speech, a conversation, or a thought in the State. Although the first university and the first public school of the country had been established in Massachusetts, the intellectual flowering of New England was to come at a later date.

For the time being, the crystal resource of water was preoccupation enough. Harnessed for manufacturing as well as for the gristmill and sawmill, waterpower was now making available hundreds of articles the colonists heretofore had had to make by hand, import from other countries, or do without. The bright day of the craftsman was almost over. But in 1822 Boston still remembered and respected the old

An early dentist in his workroom. *Gleason's Pictorial Drawing-Room Companion*, 1852.

masters—the Reveres, the Greenwoods, and the Flaggs.

Who were they, and what were they?

They were merchants, musicians, engravers, umbrella makers, ivory turners, silversmiths, soldiers and jewelers. They also made ironware, cannon, and midnight rides.

Isaac Greenwood advertised mathematical instruments, fifes and flutes, artificial legs, hands, and teeth—all in the same sentence. Moreover, in the apprenticeship pattern common to all trades, he passed along his skills to his four sons.

Paul Revere always identified himself with the occupation of gold and silversmithing, a craft allied to the work of his lifelong friend, Josiah Flagg, Sr., who was a jeweler as well as a concertmaster. These two men also produced a music book, with Flagg editing the contents and Revere making the engravings.

For six years Paul Revere made artificial teeth. After the Revolution, of which he became a legendary part, he engraved paper money and the familiar Indian of the Massachusetts seal. He concocted a mixture of copper and tin, with a touch of zinc and lead, for the making of four hundred bells, the first to be manufactured in Boston. He fitted the ship *Constitution* with copper sheathing, covered the new State House dome with copper, and started a famous industry.

All this, and dentistry too.

This diversity was not uncommon. It sometimes seemed to the harried Revere that he was expected not only to know everything, but also to do everything.

Usually he did.

As for being a dentist, the word was conveniently borrowed from the Latin *dens*, which means "tooth." The title had as many meanings as there were people to use it.

"The dentist has come," someone told an elderly farmer who was hard-of-hearing.

"The tempest—the tempest?" the old man persisted. He was no better off when told the proper word, for he did not understand its meaning. "Dentist" was especially unfamiliar to people in the country. "Pity the person in a small village with a big

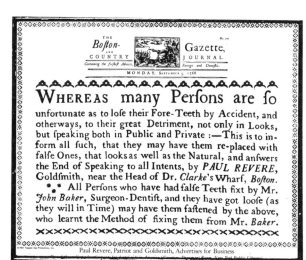

ul Revere's ad in the
ston *Gazette,* 5 Sept.
38.

toothache," wrote one of the early commentators.

In the whole country in 1800 a hundred so-called dentists could be counted. Each man had his own definition of the trade. To some it was the pulling of teeth. To others, such as the jewelers who had dexterity with delicate tools, it was the making of artificial teeth. Only to the very few medical men who specialized in oral problems was dentistry a serious practice.

These few physicians were lone voices crying in a wilderness of intentional quackery and unintentional ignorance.

Incensed at the injuries perpetrated by the "murderous hands" of the so-called dentists, these men wrote treatises and manuals by the score.

Such a publication was Josiah Flagg's *The Family Dentist,* pub-

lished in 1822, Massachusetts' first significant contribution to the dental profession. Flagg, grandson of the Josiah Flagg who was Paul Revere's friend, was well suited to write this book, since he had first studied under Dr. John C. Warren, the Boston surgeon, and had then earned a degree at the Harvard Medical School.

By the end of the eighteenth century much was known about the human teeth. Every phase of dentistry had been established, at least in theory. But dental practice lagged far behind.

This had been the tragedy of colonial dentistry.

The teeth of the American colonists were known all over the world as the worst in the world. Hardly a description of early Americans omits the horrible condition of their teeth. There was one theory that

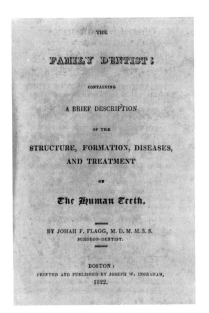

Title page of Flagg's book. *Photo courtesy of the American Antiquarian Society.*

the air in this country caused the trouble. Another insisted the tremendous breakfasts were to blame. Poor Richard pronounced the villains to be "hot soupings and frozen apples."

Ready to blame the mother country for as much as possible, a few persons supported the theory of inheritance and quoted Jeremiah to prove it: "The fathers have eaten a sour grape and the children's teeth are set on edge." Because so many babies died during teething there was thought to be some connection, but no one knew what it was. And consumption, "present everywhere, in every town, and in almost every family," was labeled as one of the "miserable consequences of bad teeth."

No country ever had so many toothless and toothaching patriots. Oliver Wendell Holmes once said that in his family the only relief for ager (the word children used for toothache) was a plaster called Dr. Oliver, presumably because his great-great-grandfather of that name had first used it. Dr. Holmes later found a list of the ingredients for this remedy, but he never could quite determine the proportions. "This," he reminisced, "was the family nostrum."

This dosing of oneself "for what ails you" was characteristic of the age. Roasted figs and bruised raisins were considered good for sore gums. For the really bad abscesses, leeches were available at the apothecary shop. Put one of these little creatures in a bottle, the sufferer was instructed, and let it down gently on the gum. Instantaneous relief was promised.

For plain, old-fashioned toothache the standbys were clove, mustard, cinnamon, peppermint, and horseradish. An extraordinarily cautious dentist advised: "If the pain is caused by heat, use cold things, and if it is the other way around, take something warm in the mouth."

If simple remedies did not work, there was always the final recourse of burning the ear.

Portrait of Josiah **Flagg**. *Photo courtesy of the Temple University School of Dentistry, Philadelphia.*

When John Greenwood, a son of Isaac Greenwood, created the slogan that "a clean tooth never decays," the country was off on the first of its crusades for hygiene. Store counters became crowded with magic formulae for cleaning teeth. One "infallible" powder promised to make teeth "white as alabaster, notwithstanding they may be black as coal."

Black as coal they well might be and commonly so covered with tartar that there were numerous instances when there seemed to be only "one tooth in each jaw, extending from ear to ear."

For brushing the teeth cold water, not hot, was recommended. After all, the teeth were thought to be bones, and everyone knows a bone when boiled will turn to glue or jelly.

Only when nothing—cleanliness, neglect, or nostrum—could help, did the colonists finally seek out the dentist. In such an extremity, there were two things to do for a bad tooth—"pull it or plug it." There were few men brave enough to plug it, but there were many strong enough to pull it.

At best, pulling teeth was an act of violence. The dentist who promised "no time for pain" may have been right about the time involved, but the sudden terror was almost unbearable. Very often the sides of the sockets came out with the tooth. Just as often the tooth was broken or crumbled.

Hemorrhaging was often profuse. Common salt or creosote, with camphor to disguise the odor, was suggested for such an emergency. If neither of these remedies worked, the alternative was to stuff the mouth with "cushions of rags" until the patient presumably stopped either bleeding or breathing.

Blacksmiths did the neatest job of pulling teeth. These versatile men, who held whole communities in the skill of their powerful hands, had the surest strength. "It's simple," said one brawny toothpuller, "just pull the tooth as if you were pulling out a nail from a horse's shoe."

43

William Lovett's portrait of Isaac Greenwood. *Photo courtesy of the New-York Historical Society, New York City.*

For many years the wearing of artificial teeth was thought to be unseemly, a "disgraceful violation of propriety." And, if anyone happened to come to this country with a gold pivot tooth, he was careful not to wear it on the Sabbath.

Women were especially susceptible to tooth disease and loss. "A tooth for every child" was a rule that could determine the size of almost any family, but the loss of teeth was considered no more serious than the loss of hair. Only vanity was involved. Sometimes the more fashionable ladies wore "plumpers," little ivory balls or pieces of beeswax to fill out the cheeks, but this was criticized as worldly. Many people cultivated the habit of holding a sprig of myrtle in the mouth to cover unsightly gaps. It has even been said

that mustaches were invented for the same reason.

The hundreds of sunken cheeks and toothless gums presented an irresistible opportunity to colonial artisans. Goldsmiths, silversmiths, tinsmiths—all adept with instruments and equipped with a knowledge of metals—were the first to make artificial teeth. These teeth were often of ivory (which soon deteriorated and caused an offensive odor), of hippopotamus tusk, or of animal bone. A few were made of "earth, hardened by heat and enameled." Also there were human teeth.

Transplantation was very popular at the time of the Revolution, and the second Josiah Flagg, the first to use the title Doctor, offered cash for healthy, handsome teeth. Dr. Greenwood called transplantation a "miserable operation," but this custom prevailed for many years. The poor sold their teeth as often as they did their hair. Once moved from one mouth to another, the teeth were purely cosmetic. No one was ever known to chew with them.

Early dental tools tell their own story of lineage. The chisels and pliers were in miniature the tools of the carpenter. Scalers were patterned after ship-building tools; the files and drills belonged to the metalsmiths. Bow drills were borrowed from the watchmaker, and the first powered drill was adapted from an old spinning wheel. The key, the familiar extracting tool, looked like nothing more than an old-fashioned door key.

Pulling and making teeth were the first steps. Setting teeth in the mouth was the next procedure. Craftsmen who attempted the first two were not timid about trying the third. "Wrap cotton around a wire, and drive it into the canal of the root," directed one brash artisan. On the other hand, cotton retains saliva and becomes offensive, so it might be better to use wood. "Well-seasoned walnut will last many years and give a surprising degree of firmness." Next, drill a hole in the under part of the crown, into which a gold screw can be placed. Of course, you *could* use walnut again. If there are no roots to which a crown can be fastened, tie the artificial tooth with thread to a natural tooth.

After such an ordeal, he added, it is not uncommon for the face to swell, and uneasiness may develop. "No blame, however, can justly fall on the dentist."

Such open revelation of procedure was not usual. Secrecy was the chief characteristic of the dentist's trade. Each man had his own formulae, tricks, and remedies, which he shared with no one—that is, unless there was adequate financial consideration.

Ethics was still an undefined word

in dentistry. And advertising, later to be forbidden by the dental profession, was a lively competition of wit and exaggeration.

"Teeth pulled while you wait," slyly observed one advertisement, as if teeth could be pulled any other way. "Pulled without pain," lied another. There is a story of an old man who boasted that being shot while hunting deer did not hurt him any more than having a tooth pulled.

"You've probably never had one pulled," retorted an experienced listener.

Pain was part of the process. When business was dull for a dentist in the western part of the State, he hired a small boy to sit in the office and yell at the top of his lungs.

"It lends an air of business to the establishment," was the logical explanation.

The first Dr. Flagg was an avid advertiser. First adopting two crossed toothbrushes as his special symbol, he then added the dramatic touch of the caduceus. He advertised a "spectacular" way of extracting nerves "simply and safely," offered all types of dental service, and suggested surgery for oral defects.

He also gave his descendants and this country its first dentist's chair. Through three subsequent generations of dentistry this chair was used, its seat of applewood warmed

Josiah Flagg's dental chair. *Photo courtesy of the Temple University School of Dentistry, Philadelphia.*

by thousands of patients, the legs and rungs (made of maple, cherry, and poplar) worn into grooves by thousands of nervous feet, and the hickory spindles literally bowed by frightened muscles as they backed away from the dentist's purposeful hand.

The adjustable headrest was made of horsehair and leather; under the right arm of the chair there was a handy instrument drawer. This old Windsor chair has never been matched for its functional and attractive simplicity. Dr. Josiah Flagg himself made the chair.

This first Doctor Flagg had been adept at pulling teeth. Captured during the War of 1812 and taken to England where he practiced for several years, he once attended a demonstration where one of the best dentists in England failed to pull a bicuspid root. Dr. Flagg reached in his pocket (where else would a dentist keep his tools?) and took out his favorite, a graver. In no time at all the root flew across the room, with Dr. Flagg explaining his theory that "two things can't occupy the same space at the same time."

One very common custom of the period was to take out an aching tool, file out the decay, fill the cavity with lead or tin, or even wood, then put the tooth back in position.

There were no standard procedures.

Like an unwanted stepchild, dentistry belonged to no one in particular. Not really a trade, it was not a profession or a business, although most physicians extracted teeth as part of their practice. Gradually another group of technicians evolved. At first they called themselves dental practitioners. Later they borrowed the term "doctor," but the title had no connection with educational background. It was an awkward age, with dentistry trying to combine the respectability of an old occupation with the naiveté of a new one.

There were no regulations, no rules, no licenses. There was not even much practical training. At best, prospective dentists spent only a few weeks of apprenticeship with an established practitioner. John Greenwood admitted that he began dentistry "out of fun" after pulling a tooth while visiting in the office of a dentist friend. "I had never seen one drawn before in all my life," he said afterwards. "It came out well and encouraged me to attempt others." ("I shall always prefer your services to those of any other," wrote Washington at a later date.)

Except in the larger settlements of the country, dental practitioners were usually itinerants. Dental treatment was still a luxury, and only the large cities could support a dentist. One country practitioner, just over the northern line of Massachusetts, reported in 1822 that he was the only dentist known from Canada to Albany and from the Rocky to the White Mountains.

A typical notice of the period began: "I travel over the entire Massachusetts area, and shall not return here for one year."

By 1822 there were fifty-one physicians in Boston. Four were listed as surgeon dentists. This was the situation, as far as dentistry was concerned, in a city of 43,000 persons. For every one of them, and their counterparts everywhere in the country, the third Josiah Flagg had a burning conscience and concern.

It was for them he wrote his little book. He planned another, a bigger book, for the practitioner, but it was never published. In many a village record, nevertheless, there is evidence that practioners made good use of *The Family Dentist*. For some Massachusetts dentists, this book was the only guide they had.

The Family Dentist was a connecting link between what had been and what was to be. While time was spanning two generations, a demand for dental service had been established. An interest had been aroused and a new practice, indigenous to this country, had been created. Looking back, it would seem to anyone that dentistry had come a considerable distance.

But there was still a long, long way to go.

"Curious, Useful & Entertaining"

by Sinclair Hitchings

Isaiah Thomas' almanac, Thomas liked to assure his readers, contained more "Matters Curious, Useful and Entertaining" than any other almanac.

The Worcester printer and publisher, who first used the phrase on the title page of his almanac for 1781, even then was in a fair way to prove it true. Many a customer must have been convinced, for scattered records show that Thomas, who sold only 3,300 copies of his almanac for 1783, had built up to an edition of 29,000 by 1797. By then his almanac was at the top of the heap in New England in a highly competitive, highly profitable field.

Thomas, the first man to make printing a really big business in this country, believed in giving his customers something extra and reminding them of it.

"As I wish to make this work truly useful to every purchaser, I have given the whole of the Act for establishing the Federal Courts in these States; an Act which every citizen ought to be acquainted with, and which of itself is sold in a pamphlet for one quarter of a dollar," readers of the almanac for 1790 were told in an unsigned note on the reverse of the title page. The almanac sold for sixpence a copy, the equivalent of about ten cents in the currency of the time. Thomas' statement was typical of his patriotism and of his attention to advertising.

The Thomas almanacs which survive from the 1780's and 90's, generally well worn, often torn, usually bearing marginal notes in the hand of the original owner, still are "curious, useful and entertaining." They have much to tell about the kind of man Thomas was, about the secret of his success, and about the New Englanders who bought his slim pocketbooks-of-the-year by the many thousands.

As a businessman, Thomas allowed himself a limited amount of space. The 1775 almanac, one of his earliest, had twenty-four pages. By 1787 it had expanded to forty-eight pages. That became its standard size.

As a publisher who liked to tell

his readers that the almanacs they were buying were worth more than the price, he packed so much useful material into his little books that sometimes he was hard pressed to find room for the curious and the entertaining. As a printer he restlessly experimented with format to see how he could get more material into the same space.

"The encouragement given to this Almanack excites my gratitude, and nothing in my power shall be wanting, whilst I continue its publication, to make it worthy your purchase," the reader was told at the beginning of the almanac for 1794. "I observe, not without satisfaction, that my arrangement respecting the Calendar pages, and the addition of many columns, &c. gives satisfaction, and as one proof of it, others have introduced the method into their publications. As a circumstance in favour of the contents of my former Almanacks, a new author has not only endeavoured to copy our shape, in size and arrangement, but has given copious extracts in his work from those which I have published for several years past, and which you will easily perceive by comparing his last year's Almanack with some of my old ones."

The "new author" was Robert B. Thomas, who was to become the dean of almanac editors and whose *Farmer's Almanac* was to become *The Old Farmer's Almanac,* still hale

Isaiah Thomas, by Ethan Allen Greenwood

and hearty today. The younger man, true enough, had gone over much of the same ground habitually covered in the Isaiah Thomas almanac. Where he had gotten his table of roads, distances, and tavern keepers, his list of courts and sessions and other tables and schedules was of course an open question; he asserted, in reply, that his almanac was no more like Thomas' than any one almanac was like another.

Competition from an almanac maker apparently born for the occupation was far from Isaiah Thomas' most difficult problem as he built up his business. He had worked through the hard years of war. Plagued by debt, the inability of many of his customers to pay, and the difficulties of obtaining type and paper, he had fought his way through successive and often unpredictable difficulties. He had issued an almanac of his own in 1775, then was unable to publish another until 1779. From that time he published every year until 1804, when his son became publisher.

Thomas, like any publisher, had to keep his writers producing, and it appears that he managed the rarer feat of making them produce according to a strict schedule. He consistently managed to get into the market early, with time enough to reprint as necessary before the new year to fill demand. "It was Thomas' custom," notes Clifford K. Shipton, his biographer, "to wring the manuscript out of the compiler in August, to begin printing in October, and to run through the second or third printing before competing almanacs began to appear in December."

Robert B. Thomas had put into his new almanac a "farmer's calendar" of advice and comment on the farmer's work and life each month of the year. This calendar was one of the reasons the younger man's almanacs were immediately successful. Isaiah Thomas recognized that the bulk of his customers, too, were farmers, and he made special efforts to cater to them — efforts which no doubt were one reason for the rapid increase in his almanac sales over many years.

The idea for the farmer's calendar, in fact, may have come from the

THOMAS's
MASSACHUSETTS, CONNECTICUT, RHODE-ISLAND, NEWHAMPSHIRE & VERMONT
ALMANACK,
With an EPHEMERIS, for the Year of Our LORD
1789:
Being the firſt Year after BISSEXTILE, or LEAP YEAR, and Thirteenth of the INDEPENDENCE of AMERICA.
From Creation, according to the Scriptures, 5751.
Fitted to the Latitude and Longitude of the Town of BOSTON, but will ſerve without eſſential Variation for the adjacent States.
Containing, beſides the MORE than uſual Aſtronomical Calculations, a larger Quantity and greater Variety, than are to be found in any other Almanack,
Of Matters Curious, Uſeful and Entertaining.

VIEW yon majeſtick concave of the ſky !
Contemplate well thoſe glorious Orbs on high—
There Conſtellations ſhine and Comets blaze ;
Each glitt'ring world the Godhead's pow'r diſplays.

Printed at WORCESTER, by ISAIAH THOMAS.
[Price 40 s. per Groſs. 4 s. per Dozen. Six Pence Single.]

"Concise Calendar for young Farmers and Gardeners" which Isaiah Thomas published in his almanac for 1786. The Calendar must have been popular, for he reprinted it in his almanacs for 1788, 1793, and 1798.

From the admonitions of the Concise Calendar a picture of the self-sufficing New England farm emerges. The prudent farmer must be hauling wood in January to store for summer fuel; must be pruning his fruit trees in February; mending

APRIL begins on *Wednesday*, hath xxx Days.

SUNSHINE intermits with ardour,
Shades fly swiftly o'er the fields,
Showers revive the drooping verdure,
Sweets the sunny upland yields.

SOLAR CALCULATIONS, &c.

Days.	☉	H	♄	♃	♂	♀	☿
1	♈ 12 22	♎ 5	♓ 14	♌ 12	♒ 21	♓ 27	♓ 15
7	18 16	6	14	12	24	♈ 4	16
13	24 8	7	14	12	27	11	23
19	29 58	8	14	11	♓ 0	18	♈ 2
25	♉ 5 49	9	13	11	3	26	14

M. D.	W. D.	Calendar, remarkable Days, Observations, &c.	☉ rise.	☉ sets.	L. D. H. M.	☉ S.
1	4	ALL FOOLS. *Contentment*	5 40	6 20	12 40	3
2	5	*lies not in the things*	5 39	6 21	12 42	3
3	6	*which we possess,*	5 38	6 22	12 44	3
4	7	St. Ambrose. *but*	5 37	6 23	12 46	2
5	D	6th in Lent. *in the*	5 36	6 24	12 48	2
6	2	Governour and Senate chosen in	5 34	6 26	12 52	2
7	3	(Massachusetts. *mind*	5 33	6 27	12 54	2
8	4	*that values them.*	5 32	6 28	12 56	1
9	5	Peace ratified by G. Britain 1784.	5 30	6 30	13 0	1
10	6	Good Frid. Christ cru. A.D. 33.	5 28	6 32	13 4	1
11	7	*Hypocrites first cheat*	5 27	6 33	13 6	1
12	D	Easter Sunday, or Christ's res-	5 26	6 34	13 8	0
13	2	(urrection.	5 25	6 35	13 10	0
14	3	*the world, and then*	5 24	6 36	13 12	0
15	4	Night's len. 10 h. 46 m.	5 23	6 37	13 14	F.
16	5	*themselves.*	5 22	6 38	13 16	0
17	6	American Independence allowed	5 20	6 40	13 20	1
18	7	(by the Dutch.	5 18	6 42	13 24	1
19	D	1st past Easter. Bat. Lex. 1775.	5 17	6 43	13 26	1
20	2	*Money is said to be*	5 15	6 45	13 30	1
21	3	*the root of all*	5 14	6 46	13 32	2
22	4	*evil, if so, we are*	5 13	6 47	13 34	2
23	5	St. George, patron of England.	5 11	6 49	13 38	2
24	6	*in a fair way of*	5 10	6 50	13 40	2
25	7	St. Mark Evang. *soon*	5 9	6 51	13 42	2
26	D	2d past Easter. *becoming*	5 7	6 53	13 46	3
27	2	*a virtuous people.*	5 6	6 54	13 48	3
28	3	*Industry and economy*	5 5	6 55	13 50	3
29	4	*will not only enrich*	5 3	6 57	13 54	3
30	5	*individuals, but societies.*	5 2	6 58	13 56	3

APRIL, Fourth Month, 1789.

LUNAR CALCULATIONS, &c.

☽ First quarter 3d day, 3d hour, morning.
● Full moon 9th day, 7th hour, evening.
☾ Last quarter 17th day, 2d hour, morning.
○ New moon 25th day, 5th hour, morning.

M. D.	W. D.	Tides, Aspects, Weather, &c.	● A.	High Water, morn.	& eve.	● pl.	● rise & sets.	● sou. H. M.
1	4	☉ ♃ △	6	4 7	3 40	♊	morn.	4 52
2	5	Now	7	5 1	4 34	♋	0 32	5 46
3	6	Low Tides.	8	6 0	5 32	♋	1 21	6 45
4	7	(☊ 18°. ♏	9	6 57	6 27	♌	2 7	7 42
5	D	look out	10	7 52	7 22	♌	2 48	8 37
6	2	☽ Perigee.	11	8 49	8 19	♍	3 26	9 34
7	3	☽ ♄ ☍	12	9 36	9 6	♍	4 4	10 21
8	4	7*s set 9 h. 45 m.	13	10 26	9 56	♎	4 29	11 11
9	5	High Tides.	⊕	11 28	10 58	♎	☽ rise.	morn.
10	6	for	15	morn.	11 48	♏	6 36	0 6
11	7	rain	16	0 17	E. 37	♏	7 54	1 2
12	D	or	17	1 10	1 30	♏	9 0	1 55
13	2	snow.	18	2 6	2 26	♐	10 5	2 51
14	3	☉ ♀ △	19	3 0	3 26	♐	11 0	3 45
15	4	High	20	3 52	4 22	♑	11 47	4 37
16	5	winds	21	4 48	5 14	♑	morn.	5 33
17	6	Low Tides.	22	5 40	6 6	♒	0 33	6 33
18	7	in	23	6 26	6 52	♒	1 21	7 15
19	D	many	24	7 12	7 40	♒	1 47	7 57
20	2	☽ Apogee.	25	7 55	8 23	♓	2 16	8 40
21	3	7*s set 8 h. 57 m.	26	8 41	9 9	♓	2 40	9 26
22	4	places.	27	9 23	9 43	♈	3 10	10 8
23	5	☊ 14°. ♌	28	10 5	10 26	♈	3 34	10 50
24	6	♅ ☿ st.	29	10 47	11 8	♈	4 1	11 32
25	7	The	○	11 29	11 51	♉	☽ sets.	E. 14
26	D	spring	1	E. 11	morn.	♉	7 29	1 1
27	2	Middling Tides.	2	1 8	0 39	♊	8 31	1 53
28	3	advances.	3	2 6	1 34	♊	9 33	2 51
29	4	Fair.	4	3 1	2 31	♋	10 31	3 47
30	5	Cloudy.	5	3 58	3 30	♋	11 26	4 43

C

fences in March; turning ground and planting in April; planting in May, "a very busy month for Farmers and Gardeners"; hoeing and weeding in June, and sowing, too; sowing some more in July, and mowing, weeding, and watering; reaping and mowing "all kinds of corn [grain]" in August; drying stalks of Indian corn for fodder and digging potatoes in September; gathering Indian corn and husking it and making cider ("No time in this month must be lost") in October; storing vegetables and moving the animals and bees under shelter in November; and in December repairing and grinding tools, killing hogs and fat cattle, and taking time in the long evenings for reading and "social hours."

These are only a few of the jobs the farmer is admonished to look after. The calendar touches everything from planting flax to caring for pigeons and minding an herb garden. It was well named the Concise Calendar, for it wasted no words. There was room, however, for a

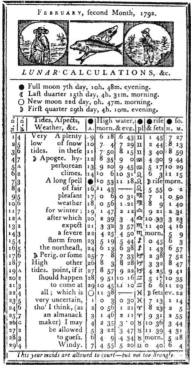

LUNAR·CALCULATIONS,·&c.

● Full moon 7th day, 10h. 48m. evening.
☾ Laſt quarter 15th day, 4h. 31m. morning.
○ New moon 22d day, 0h. 47m. morning.
☽ Firſt quarter 29th day, 4h. 10m. evening.

D. M.	D. W.	Tides, Aſpects, Weather, &c.	● A.	High water, morn. & eve.	● pl	● riſe & ſets	● ſo. H. M.
1	4	Very A plenty	9	6 18 6 43	♊	1 45	7 27
2	5	low of ſnow	10	7. 4 7 29	♊	2 44	8 13
3	6	tides. in theſe	11	7 50 8 15	♊	3 40	8 59
4	7	☽ Apogee. hy-	12	8 35 9 0	♋	4 30	9 44
5	A	perborean	13	9 20 9 45	♋	5 17	10 29
6	2	climes.	14	10 6 10 31	♌	6 3	11 15
7	3	A long ſpell	●	10 53 11 18	♌	☽ riſe	morn.
8	4	of fair	16	11 43 ――	♌	5 55	0 2
9	5	pleaſant	17	0 6 0 31	♍	7 1	0 50
10	6	weather	18	0 56 1.21	♍	8 9	1 40
11	7	for winter ;	19	1 47 2 12	♍	9 21	2 31
12	A	after which	20	2 39 3 4	♎	10 33	3 23
13	2	expect	21	3 32 3 57	♏	11 40	4 16
14	3	a ſevere	22	4 25 4 50	♏	morn.	5 9
15	4	ſtorm from	23	5 19 5 44	♐	0 45	6 3
16	5	the northeaſt,	24	6 13 6 38	♐	1 43	6 57
17	6	☽ Perig. or ſome	25	7 8 7 33	♑	2 38	7 52
18	7	High other	26	8 3 8 28	♑	3 32	8 47
19	A	tides. point, if it	27	8 57 9 22	♑	4 25	9 41
20	2	ſhould happen	28	9 51 10 16	♒	5 17	10 35
21	3	to come at	29	10 45 11 10	♒	6 6	11 29
22	4	all ; which is	○	11 38 ――	♓	☽ ſets	ev. 22
23	5	very uncertain,	1	0 3 0 30	♓	7 13	1 14
24	6	tho' I think, (as	2	0 56 1 21	♈	8 23	2 5
25	7	an almanack	3	1 46 2 11	♈	9 31	2 55
26	G	maker) I may	4	2 35 3 0	♉	10 36	3 44
27	2	be allowed	5	3 22 3 47	♉	11 39	4 31
28	3	to gueſs.	6	4 9 4 34	♉	morn.	5 18
29	4	Windy.	7	4 55 5 20	♊	0 40	6 4

This year maids are allowed to court—but not too ſtrongly.

mournful sigh over New England weather. In the remarks for March the writer noted: "The seasons are so uncertain in this country, as to their approach, that it is needless to say when the particular week should be to begin particular farming business — it is best to watch the weather, and be prepared to begin your work when it will permit."

Every Isaiah Thomas almanac, of course, contained weather prophecies. Once, at least, the weather prophet dropped his guard and

made something very like a confession. His prediction, on one of the calendar pages of the almanac for 1792, covered the period from February 7 to February 28: "A long spell of fair pleasant weather for winter; after which expect a severe storm from the northeast, or some other point, if it should happen to come at all; which is very uncertain, tho' I think (as an almanack maker) I may be allowed to guess."

The man who was compiling Thomas' almanacs at this time was Daniel George of Portland. It was George who finally persuaded Thomas to dispense with astrological sections which had been fixtures year after year. In a letter to Thomas he inveighed against "the nonsensical jargon of astrologers and fortune-tellers."

It is hard to distinguish between the work of the compiler and Thomas' own work on the almanac. Thomas was probably the author of the addresses to the reader printed on the reverse of the almanac's title page. These addresses, beginning "Kind Reader" or "Courteous Reader," were first signed "Philomathes," later "The Editor"; some carried no signature.

With patriotism and faith in his readers, Thomas printed documents that reflected the emergence of the United States. The Articles of Confederation were in his almanac for 1783, the articles of peace between

America and Great Britain in his almanac for 1784, along with the substance of the Massachusetts constitution. His almanac for 1786 contained the Massachusetts Bill of Rights; his almanac for 1788 had four and a half pages in tiny type devoted to proceedings of the Constitutional Convention at Philadelphia, and these only begin the list.

The compilers whom Thomas paid to make his astronomical calculations and gather other material for the almanac were learned and ingenious men, and, like Daniel George, decidedly individualists. Benjamin West of Providence, after he had completed the astronomical calculations for the almanac of 1785, wrote Thomas: "I have sent by Dr. Green, agreeably to your request, a Copy — 85; it is complete, and great Labour hath been bestow'd upon it, and a better Calculation does not come from the hands of a Doctor Maskelyne, or any of his assistants." Under his signature as an afterthought he added: "P. S. By the first safe conveyance, it will be best to send the money,... the only grease that keeps the wheels moving now a days."

Many of the features of Thomas' almanacs were standard in New England almanacs of the time. He packed in his material tightly, however; some of his competitors spread theirs thin. He also set out to do things better than the others. He called the reader's attention to the care with which he had revised his list of roads. He compiled a special list of court sessions as, "Thomas's Lawyers' and Justices' Calendar."

As Clifford K. Shipton has remarked, there was in the almanac something for everyone. There were jokes, bits of philosophy, maxims, stories, descriptions of horrors and strange phenomena, paragraphs of how-to-do-it and of tried and true home remedies. There were verses, puzzles, and astrological lore. There were useful tables and schedules, and there were the calendar pages.

The late 1780's and the 90's were the heyday of the almanac under Thomas' ownership. To modern readers who may come back to them, these well-thumbed volumes contain much of the character of New England in that decade. Boston is revealed as the hub of the universe in these handy little pocketbooks, but in the tables for travelers the roads reach from that starting point into the far corners of the newly-United States. The center of society is the family farm, where Thomas' trusted almanac, a string threaded through one corner, hung in the kitchen for ready reference.

Work hard, the almanacs urge; mind your business and your morals, and you will prosper. Mind your almanac, too, and the familiar injunction in the December calendar: "Sew this Almanack to your old ones, and buy a new one."

Godspeed to the Plough

by Marise Fawsett

One of the oldest houses on Cape Cod is located so far from the beaten path that anyone not really familiar with the area would never know it existed. A paved road borders part of the property, and from there a narrow lane winds down a considerable distance through some woods to a broad clearing beside a pond. There it is, the old Percival homestead in South Sandwich. It was built at least 250 years ago, possibly quite a bit earlier, because there were Percivals in Sandwich almost from the time the town was founded. Early church records report the birth of Elizabeth Percival, daughter of James Percival, in 1675. They were a prolific family. An impressive number of Percivals lived and died in Sandwich over a very long period, though none by that name are now left on the Cape. As the families multiplied they fanned out around Sandwich, and some bought farms in neighboring towns.

Subsequent owners have modernized the Percival house at different times and added onto it. There is no trace left of the old barn and outbuildings—where they stood is now only a smooth expanse of lawn. Nevertheless, a good deal is essentially unchanged. The basic lines of the old house are still discernable, despite the additions. That ancient, hand-hewn granite stepping stone at the front door, how many, many generations of Percivals have passed over it! And those two big elms in the yard date back at least 150 years. The broad clearing around the house is bordered by woods, and so is the pond—a far cry from the virgin forest the first Percivals saw, but trees nevertheless and plenty of them. Best of all, there is no busy highway close by, no jarring sight or sound of traffic—the place is much too sequestered. A bird sings, or a squirrel snaps a twig as it scampers through a tree, or a fish jumps out in the pond. Otherwise everything is still.

These are the same sights and sounds Benjamin Percival knew when he lived and farmed that land 200 years ago. He kept a diary off and on, starting in 1777 when he was twenty-five years old. He had married Lydia Goodspeed from Barnstable, and by then had two little boys, John and Joseph. That was just the beginning; in all they would have

The pond.

ten children, including eight boys: John, Joseph, Elisha, Benjamin, Nabby, William, Josiah, Timothy, Sylvanus, and Harriet. You could hardly have too many children if you lived on a farm; every helping hand was a Godsend.

Mr. Percival was not a loquacious man; in fact, most of the diary entries are brief to the point of terseness, but they tell a good deal about what it was like to live on the Cape and be a farmer. Some of the events he took the trouble to record may not sound at all important to us:

August 27 1777 we found a Ripe Red Cherry upon one of the cherry trees today

March 27 1778 John Streeter has been here today with Pins and Combs to sell

Nov 21st 1778 the wild geese begin to fly over

Jan 29th 1779 I saw a Dear out to the head of our orchard

But they were important to him, and his interest in everyday things is a part of the picture. The average eighteenth-century American farmer and his family (ninety per cent of the population were then farmers) had little contact with the world at large. There were only a few newspapers in the entire country, and their circulation was confined for the most part to the towns where they were published. Delivering a letter or newspaper any distance meant waiting until someone was "riding that way" and would take it along. There was no real postal service in this country until late in the century; Cape Cod's first mail service was set up between Barnstable and Boston in 1792, when a local resident was appointed to make the round trip once a week on horseback, carrying the mail each way in his saddlebags. There weren't any stagecoaches on the Cape before 1790. In short, news

The Percival house today.

from the outside was slow to arrive, sporadic, and unreliable. It is no wonder that local items like the weather, crops, neighbors, migrating geese, even a ripe cherry several weeks out of season loomed so large.

Births, deaths, and marriages were faithfully recorded in the diary. Some of the entries are chilling:

March 11th 1779 Paul Jones Wife hanged her Self today apple trees begin to flower

He was just as terse when he recorded the death of his son Josiah:

Feb 4th 1803 this day Josiah Percival was Drowned having fell in while skating on the ice

Feb 7th 1803 this day Josiah Percival was buried a great many people attended his funeral he was 13 years old the 8th day of October

One can imagine the heartbreak that lay behind those few, stoical

words. Like an iceberg, only a small part showed.

Every kind of business transaction was recorded, and there were a great many. They range in importance from a sizable purchase of land adjoining his farm, to the sale of some sheep or an ox, to bartering two quarts of molasses for a peck of rye.

Benjamin Percival served as Selectman in Sandwich for twenty years and there are frequent references to town affairs, most of them too brief to be illuminating. Sandwich had no Town Hall in those days, much less a Selectmen's office. Town meetings were held in the Meetinghouse, or in the back room of the General Store. The Selectmen did much of their work at home and met together in one another's houses. They must have spent a good deal of time in the saddle too, riding about on town business. The Percival farm in South Sandwich was probably seven or eight miles from Sandwich center (since there were different roads then, it is hard to tell exactly). Just going in to Sandwich Village and back sounds like a bit of an undertaking, with nothing swifter than a horse to get you there, and never mind the weather. What severe weather could mean if one had to get around in it is broûght home by the following entry:

March 19th 1817 T got home from Falmouth to day horse badly froze afraid die

Old-time farmers had to be out in all weather and at all hours, and a constant awareness of nature was essential to their calling. Mr. Percival was a practical man, and a busy man, but he was never too engaged to note the first robins, the first spring peepers, the first apple, pear, and cherry blossoms, the first winter night the pond froze over:

April 16 1790 got home from Scorton almost noon the grass has started so that Cattle graze and grow Dainty about eating fodder been a warm day saw a Snake to Day

March 11 1791 I saw Robin Ruks to Day first I have seen

April 24 1791 today has been Remarkable for a Snow Storm it looked Strange to see fiefingers and violets covered with Snow

The term "Robin Ruks" which appears often in the diary dates back to pre-Elizabethan England. "Ruk" was "a heap or stack of fuel or combustible material"—hence "robin ruk" was the Middle English equivalent of our "robin redbreast." It was one of many terms the early settlers brought with them from seventeenth-century England which lingered on for a few generations. Another example is "pompion" for pumpkin:

November 11 1777 . . . and Securing our Pompions from the Inclemencies of old Rigged [sic] winter which seems to be approaching upon us in full correer whether prepared or not

Shakespeare uses the word "pumpion" in the "Merry Wives of Windsor."

"Fiefingers" in the previous entry is, of course, Five Fingers or Cinquefoil (*Potentilla Simplex*), a common weed with small yellow flowers that blooms from April to August and is abundant on the Cape and throughout New England. Each leaf is composed of five leaflets, hence the name. The plant is small and low-growing with numerous runners, like the strawberry. It thrives in good soil but seems equally partial to barren, cut-over places, where it valiantly attempts to cover the bare ground with its runners as if driven by some Victorian sense of propriety.

There was no generation gap in early America. Traditional centuries-old methods of farming were handed down intact from father to son with almost no change. Each farm with its varied crops and different kinds of livestock was a self-sustaining unit. The farmer and his family worked closely together to produce everything they needed—food, shelter, heat, and clothing. They often forged their own tools. When there was a surplus of anything they took it to the general store and exchanged it for the few commodities they could not produce themselves, such as tea, coffee, cotton goods, spices, and rum.

Thus Benjamin Percival was a jack-of-all-trades, as he had to be. One is impressed by the many tasks and skills mentioned in the diary —and they were only a few of the many chores he did since obviously he didn't bother to write everything down. Here is a sampling:

1777 Jan 30 I have been a mending Shoes

Feb 5 I have been a Swingling Flax this forenoon

March 4 we have been a sorting our sheep from strays

May 29 we have been a Splitting Stref for a cosway we have found a nest of hawks

Aug 15 I have been a making Cyder our folks have been a beating flax seed.

Aug 21 I have been down to Jeremiah Bacon's this forenoon to help make a Scythe

1778 June 29 have been a Setting of post and Rail fence between Gershom Crocker and we toward Triangle Pond

1779 Jan 25 I have been making a Swingling knife

Jan 30 have been making a nue fence between Jos Lawrence and us we made the fence by falling trees one upon another

Feb 15 this afternoon have cut a tree for cart sides

Feb 22 is a stormy day have made a hogs trough went to ploughing in the afternoon but got catcht in the Rain and quitted it has been a very hard rain

1788 Jan 28 today we have been Cutting a nue Road to go to town

June 10 yesterday we went to Peleg Hoxies to help raise his barn

1789 March 23 today we have been Snaking logs and mortising posts and sowd some hay Seed upon the Snow

July 15 last week split rails I split out one tree that made 26 rails 14 out one way and 12 out the other

Nov 27 last Monday we went to help move Isaiah Marston's house we had upwards of 30 yoke of oxen broke one cable in two or three places and finally had not strength to draw it more than 2 or 3 rods.

Dec 4 yesterday morning was a

storm after it held up we went to help move Isaiah Marston's house again we got it 30 or 40 rods and left it again they moved it the day before about half a mile

But it wasn't all work. Occasionally an entry sounds quite jolly:

1777 March 27 I have been to Anne Goodspeeds wedding

March 28 come home from wedding with some of the weddeners with me

Nov 4 we have had a grand husking this evening about 70 or 80 people I believe husked about 10 Load of Corn in good season

Corn huskings, like barn and house raisings, were a pleasant and effective way to get a big job done. Friends and neighbors came from miles around and made short work of it; in return they could count on the same kind of help when they needed it. Meantime, for an immediate reward, there was plenty of rum and cider and good things to eat. And sometimes there was music and dancing afterwards in the big barn.

Benjamin Percival was twenty-three years old when the Revolutionary War broke out. He joined the Sandwich militia and made regular trips in to the village for drilling. "Went to training," which appears here and there in the diary, meant a long jog on horseback. Most farm chores for that day just had to wait. But for the younger men especially it must have been an exciting break from routine.

When the British took over Provincetown and Truro as a convenient base of naval operations, war became a reality for Cape Cod. Its shipping was crippled as the surrounding waters were controlled by the enemy. Its younger men were constantly being ordered inland to engage in fighting, which put a heavy burden on those who had to struggle along at home short-handed. Farmers suffered severely when their horses and cattle were continually requisitioned for the Continental Army or captured by enemy forays. On April 2nd, 1777 Cape Cod nearly experienced actual combat; ten British vessels attacked Falmouth, intending to burn it as a warning to other rebellious Cape towns. Luckily Falmouth had sufficient warning to summon reinforcements from Sandwich. When landing parties from the British ships approached under cover of a barrage of cannon fire, the local forces they confronted were so substantial that they turned around and rowed back to their vessels. The mission was resumed the following day, but with no better success. Falmouth sustained little damage from the bombardment—most of the cannonfire had been directed at the American entrenchments part way between the town and the beach.

Benjamin Percival and his brother Thomas accompanied the

59

Sandwich militia to Falmouth:

Friday April 2nd this Evening there was an alarm to go to Falmouth there being a number of vessels seen coming Down Sound

Saturday April 3rd this morning Thos set out for Falmouth we Ploughed this forenoon and afternoon hearing heavy Cannon towards Falmouth I set out and got there just after the firing ceased our people stood it out in a Small intrenchment amidst the insesent fire from 10 armed vessels manned with Tories I did not get there till it was over they tried to land with their boats but got beat off

Sunday April 4th I staid in the guard house last night almost to the Shoar this morning the Vessels came within musket shot of our entrenchment and fired again we returned the fire they soon quitted and went to Naushon where they killed some Cattle and hogs and Left them on the Spot we hear that we wounded Some of them have picked up a great many of their balls and grape Shot some lead 4 pounders

Monday April 5th it was a Stormy night last night this morning the vessels came to Sail and proceeded to the Eastward toward Nantucket and about noon we were all Discharged and Came home

Farming, like time and the tide, waits for no man. The next day Benjamin was back again at his chores:

Tuesday April 6th have been plowing this forenoon and have been to town to mill and have plough Irons sharpened

Benjamin Percival was no ordinary farmer. In addition to his long tenure as Selectman, he served at least five years as Representative from Sandwich to the General Court in Boston. Nevertheless it seems evident from his diary that the farm which literally fed and clothed him and his family was his closest and most abiding concern. It was his way of life, just as it had been his father's and his grandfather's. And it was a good life. The following old poem celebrates the independence, self-reliance, and essential well-being of those early farmers:

GODSPEED TO THE PLOUGH

Let the Wealthy and Great
Roll in splendor and State
I envy them not I declare it;
I eat my own Lamb
My own Chicken and Ham
I shear my own Fleece and I
    wear it;
I have Lawns I have Bowers
I have Fruits I have Flowers,
The Lark is my Morning alarmer
So my jolly Boys now
Here's Godspeed to the Plough,
Long Life and Success to the
    Farmer.

The Lionhearted General

by Martha F. Child

There were 15,000 persons at General Nathaniel Lyon's funeral in the remote little hill town of Eastford, Connecticut. Three governors were there on that beautiful September day in 1861, a United States Senator, Congressman, judges, and assorted other dignitaries. General Lyon was the first northern general killed in the Civil War.

Nathaniel Lyon was born on a rocky farm in the Pilfershire District of Eastford on July 14, 1818, the seventh of nine children born to Amasa and Keziah (Knowlton) Lyon. According to tradition, Pilfershire District was so named because of the proclivities of those who had lived there at one time. Since they kept neither livestock nor poultry and their tables were plentifully supplied with meat, it was assumed their goods were pilfered from neighboring farms.

The Lyon family struggled to make a living on the rocky terrain that added to the hardships suffered by farmers of that era. The night before he was killed, as he prepared to make his bed between two rocks, General Lyon remarked that he "had been born between two rocks."

Nathaniel Lyon's great-uncle, Colonel Thomas Knowlton, led to Lexington a company of men from Ashford, the first organized body of troops going from a sister colony to the aid of Massachusetts. He was killed at the Battle of Harlem Heights and of him General Washington said in the general orders of the next day, "He would have been an honor to any country."

Lt. Daniel Knowlton, brother of Colonel Knowlton, was Nathaniel Lyon's maternal grandfather. General Israel Putnam, his companion in several French and Indian campaigns, said of him, "Such is his courage and want of fear I could order him into the mouth of a loaded cannon." When Colonel Knowlton took his men to Lexington, General Putnam asked where Daniel was, and, on being informed that he had gone in another direction, said, "I am very sorry you did not bring him with you; he alone is worth half a company."

Nurtured on stories of his illustrious relatives, Nathaniel Lyon naturally was interested in patriotic and martial exploits. Short, red haired, and tempestuous by nature, his ambition, expressed early and often, was to go to West Point. He had a Puritan upbringing. He was graduated at the district school in Eastford just a few months before entering West Point, but in the interim attended the academy at Brooklyn, Connecticut, for a few months. He was eleventh in his graduating class of fifty-two at West Point; the class had numbered over a hundred when they entered in 1837.

On July 1, 1841, he was named Second Lieutenant in the Second Regiment of Infantry. He left home in November to join his regiment, then engaged in fighting the Seminole Indians in Florida. Civilian employees of the government gave secret aid to the enemy; interpreters and guides sold ammunition to the Indians and repeated stories of designing whites; and the Spaniards on the coast circulated lies about both sides. Nathaniel Lyon disliked this assignment.

In May 1842 his regiment was sent to Sackets Harbor on Lake Ontario, where they stayed for several years. He referred to this as the easiest portion of his life. He enjoyed himself, dividing his time among military duties, studies, and the pleasures of society. Formal balls in town and parties in garrison were pleasant; he attended church twice on Sunday and once during the week; in other leisure hours he studied law and investigated Mesmerism.

Nathaniel Lyon was opposed to the annexation of Texas, fearing it would lead to war with Mexico, and it did. During the summer of 1846, he and his regiment were sent to Mexico. In February of the next year he was promoted to First Lieutenant and later in the same year to Brevet Captain, "for gallant and meritorious conduct in the Battles of Contreras and Charabusco."

In April 1849 Lyon's regiment was transferred to California, their object "to protect the inhabitants from the Indians." He referred to this stint as laborious and wearisome; hardship and privation were his constant companions in the next few years.

He was made a full Captain in June 1851 by regular promotion.

In January 1852, Nathaniel Lyon received word from home that his mother was failing in mind and body. Devoted to both parents, he was strongly attached to his mother. His father had died in 1843. He started at once on the long, tiresome journey to Connecticut, but his mother died before he arrived, and he spent the next ten months travelling. He rejoined his regiment at Fort Miller, California, in November.

Lyon was distressed by the things which had been happening in Kansas. He planned to resign his commission if he were ordered there to aid in enforcing laws enacted by the pro-slavery legislature, which owed its election to non-resident voters. Instead he was ordered to the Territory of Nebraska and in March 1857 to Sioux City, Iowa. In June of that year, having obtained another leave of absence, Lyon went east on what was to be his last visit to the scenes of his early life. In December he returned to St. Louis, and several assignments in Missouri followed.

In that era, army officers were free to deliver fiery political speeches and write violent and partisan political articles for publication. During a leave in 1860 and part of 1861, Nathaniel Lyon wrote political articles for the *Manhattan Kansas Express* and delivered many political speeches. He bitterly condemned Douglas; he "regarded with the utmost impatience the supineness of President Buchanan" and referred to him as a "blue-eyed old hypocrite." Although a Democrat, he praised Lincoln and the Republican Party, conferring frequently and confidentially with Francis Preston Blair, Jr., and other Republican leaders.

As the Civil War came closer, he made the comment which could be made of any war: "Reason seemed dethroned."

For a brief period after Lincoln was inaugurated, Lyon, fearful that war could not be avoided, was apprehensive that the President lacked the resolution necessary to deal with and put down treason forever.

In the spring of 1861, Claiborne Jackson, an ardent secessionist, took office as Governor of Missouri. A committee of Unionists was formed, armed with rifles bought by Francis P. Blair, Jr., and Samuel Filley, a local merchant. Most of the money the committee raised came from outside the state. The Secessionists organized and St. Louis was divided into two camps by these groups.

When Captain Lyon, a vigorous

abolitionist, arrived with a company of regulars, he took quarters in the Arsenal and assumed the right of command as officer of highest rank in the line. Major Peter V. Hagner, of the Ordinance Department, claimed command because of his brevet rank. Lyon believed that if Missouri passed a secession ordinance, the Governor would demand surrender of the Arsenal, and he knew the Major's defenses were inadequate. General William S. Harney was the commanding officer in St. Louis and he and Captain Lyon clashed constantly. Francis Blair's brother was Montgomery Blair, Postmaster General, and through their intercession, Lyon was appointed Brigadier General on May 17, 1861. On May 31 he replaced Harney in command.

Missouri had been made part of McClellan's Department of the Ohio, an awkward and inefficient arrangement, but on July 3, 1861, Missouri was included in the Department of the West with John Frémont in charge.

During June and July Lyon moved his men to the southwest portion of the state and the Union forces won a few small skirmishes. By the beginning of August, Lyon's men were deployed near Springfield and the Confederate Generals Price and McCulloch were coming north to fight him.

Lyon's forces grew weaker by the day, volunteers who had signed up for three months returning home because they had not been paid and their families were suffering. They were short of food and clothing and, although General Lyon called repeatedly for reinforcements, General Frémont did not respond.

It was hot; streams and wells were dry; fine dust was everywhere. Provender was so scarce that on August 4 Lyon decided to return to Springfield proper. A few days later a council of war was held and almost unanimously the officers favored the evacuation of Springfield. One officer dissented and Lyon agreed with him.

If the rebels could have been persuaded to attack him, Lyon would have been in a more favorable position strategically. Colonel Franz Sigel proposed a plan, to which Lyon unwisely agreed, to split the Union forces, with Sigel taking 1,200 of the available 5,400 men, to attack the Rebels in the rear while Lyon attacked the front. His officers strongly protested this plan, but, although he should have known better, Lyon was adamant. He was aware that Sigel might not fight if not given his own way and, in addition, he overestimated Sigel's abilities.

Lyon and his men marched out at 5:00 P.M. and about 1:00 A.M. could see the Rebel campfires. They slept in the rain until daybreak and reached the Rebel outpost at Wilson's Creek about 4:00 A.M. One of the enemy brigades tried to stop the Union advance but was driven back. When Price's men started up the hill, Lyon's men started down and they fought in a line about a mile long and at a range of fifty yards. The Rebels were driven off, but a lull in the fighting gave both sides time to re-group and fierce fighting ensued. Lyon moved along the lines, shouting encouragement. His horse was shot and he was wounded in the ankle, thigh, and scalp. Friends urged him to have the wounds attended to, but the situation was perilous and he placed himself at the head of the column. A contemporary account relates, "Inspired with almost superhuman energy by the heroics of their chief, the men rushed forward, scattering the enemy like chaff."

Lyon was hit, fell from his horse, and died a few seconds later in the arms of his orderly.

Much had been accomplished with a mathematically inferior force, the Confederates numbering slightly over ten thousand, but General Lyon by personally leading the charge in which he lost his life jeopardized the Union chances because the troops were left without a commander.

In this, one of the bloodiest one-day battles of the entire war, the killed, wounded, and missing total-led seventeen per cent of those fighting. At Antietam the loss was slightly over eighteen per cent.

Sigel distinguished himself by his ineptness on his mission, then deserted his men and ran from battle.

Before noon, with Major Samuel Sturgis in command of the Union forces, the Rebels had been driven down the hill. He did not take the risk of pursuing, however, and began the orderly retreat to Springfield, about twelve miles away.

While the Confederate commanders quarreled, the Union forces continued their orderly retreat until Sigel, outranking Sturgis, assumed command and continued the retreat toward Rolla. When he managed to disorganize the retreat, some of the officers asked Sturgis to replace him, which he did, his Regular Army rank being higher than Sigel's.

It was said that this battle might have had better results if General Frémont, commander of Union forces, had been a better general than explorer and if the troops had been better fed, trained, and paid.

In the light of all the information uncovered in the last hundred years, experts agree that the Battle of Wilson's Creek decided the course of the War in the West and was not a Union defeat. It might be considered a draw, but after it there was no chance of the State of Missouri going to the Secessionists. What Lyon might have done if he had lived no one can know, but the soldiers who fought under him were convinced they were victorious. They stood up to and beat back vastly superior forces. Grant's successful campaign on the lower Mississippi could not have been accomplished if in 1862 Missouri had not been in Union control.

General Lyon's body was placed in an ambulance on the battlefield, was temporarily removed to make way for wounded, and inadvertently was left behind in the haste of retreat. When the troops reached Springfield and discovered the body was missing, a flag of truce was sent back to the battlefield and it was recovered.

When Springfield was abandoned, again the body of General Lyon was left behind. The day after the battle, the wife of Colonel Phelps, a Union Congressman, asked permission to bury the body. It was placed in a wooden coffin enclosed in zinc and hermetically sealed. Mrs. Phelps had it put in an outdoor cellar on her farm and covered with straw. Later, fearful that it might be mutilated by soldiers, she had it buried at night. Major Sturgis, who took command of the Union forces the first day of the retreat, assumed the remains were with the troops and did not discover the truth until he was twenty-five miles from Springfield.

Although his death occurred on August 10, 1861, it was August 14 before the news of General Lyon's death became known throughout the country. His cousin, Danford Knowlton of New York City, and his brother-in-law, John B. Hasler of Webster, Massachusetts, left New York on August 15 to bring home the body of the dead hero. When they reached St. Louis on the 18th and found the body was not there, they went to Springfield, where General Frémont furnished the necessary papers for them to proceed.

They spent the night at a camp at Rolla, where a Confederate officer, there to effect an exchange of prisoners, volunteered his services to the General's relatives and gave them valuable assistance. They still had over a hundred miles to go through barren, dreary country. Upon learning the object of their journey, Confederates at outposts were extremely polite. Strange as it seems that enemies were so kindly disposed, many Confederate and Union officers alike were West Point graduates; many close friends now had to consider each other enemies.

On August 22, Mr. Knowlton and Mr. Hasler presented the communication from General Frémont to Confederate General Price, who threw the paper aside contemptuously because it was addressed "To Whom it May Concern." Nevertheless, he granted them every facility for procuring the remains.

The body was disinterred at the

Phelps farm where Mrs. Phelps extended gracious hospitality to the relatives of General Lyon. According to a contemporary account, "Everywhere within the lines of the enemy, the Secessionists treated them with distinguished kindness, attention, and courtesy, even tendering a military escort for the body from St. Louis, which was declined."

Arriving in St. Louis on the 28th of August, they remained overnight in order to allow time for a suitable demonstration, at the request of General Frémont. The next day the body was delivered at the depot to the Adams Express Company, to be conveyed east with a military escort. General Lyon's relatives had accepted the offer of the express company to carry the body and escort free of charge from St. Louis to place of burial. Separate cars were provided for the exclusive use of the escorts.

At Cincinnati and Philadelphia, military honors were accorded the General, and in New York City his body lay in state for three days in the Governor's Room. Flags in the city and on the shipping in the harbor were at half mast.

In Hartford, the body was removed from the train to the Senate Chamber of the State House, guns were fired, the State House bell was tolled, and the band played a dirge. Several military companies and a large number of citizens joined the escort. Then a special train took the body to Willimantic.

The journey from Willimantic to Eastford, about fourteen miles, was by carriage and other vehicles furnished by the people of the area.

It was dark by the time the throngs arrived in Eastford. Residents lighted their way to the hill to the Congregational Church with candles and lanterns. The City Guard of Hartford was left at the church in charge of General Lyon's body. The strangers found hospitality in the homes of the inhabitants, and Eastford House, which is now called the General Lyon Inn and is still furnishing hospitality, was headquarters for the dignitaries.

On September 5, a beautiful autumn day, the funeral services were conducted. This town of only 1,000 population at that time, was host that day to an estimated 15,000 persons.

On the coffin were placed the hat General Lyon had waved when rallying his soldiers at Wilson's Creek, and his sword and belt.

In front of the church, on the slope of the hill, a large platform had been erected for speakers and invited guests and at the foot of the platform there were benches for the use of relatives, the escort, and the military.

Ex-Governor Cleveland of Connecticut, president of the day, called the assembly to order and a choir sang a hymn, after which a former minister of the church offered a prayer. The next speaker was the Hon. Elisha Carpenter, a judge of the Superior Court, born in Eastford, who delivered an elaborate historical address, tracing General Lyon's career from childhood to Wilson's Creek. The next speaker was Congressman Galusha A. Grow of Pennsylvania, also born in Eastford, who orated at length. Governors Buckingham of Connecticut and Sprague of Rhode Island spoke, as well as a Senator, a Mayor Deming, and others.

The program ended, the people dispersed for refreshment. Huge baskets of "provender" had accompanied the expedition. A contemporary newspaper account states, "The military and guests were marched to a grove and collated." The same paper reported that pickpockets were at the funeral but knew the Hartford police were around and were therefore wary.

General Lyon had made known his wish to lie in death in the cemetery where his mother and father were buried. The funeral procession, one-and-a-half miles long, set out for the Phoenixville Cemetery. The order of march was as follows: One hundred horsemen; Tiger Engine Co. No. 7 of Southbridge, Massachusetts; Home Guard of Woodstock; Band; Light Guard of Hartford; Colt's Army Band; Hearse; City Guard of Hartford; Pall Bearers; Army and Navy Officers; Principal

relatives of deceased and mourners; Citizens on foot; Citizens in carriages. Fitting ceremonies were conducted at the grave.

And there he rests. Credited by historians and the people of Missouri with having saved the state for the Union, Missouri has honored him in several ways. There is a bronze statue of General Lyon in Lyon Park, near the St. Louis Arsenal; Jefferson City is the site of a monument; in St. Louis is a school named for him.

Not so the state and town where he was born, grew up, and returned to after a hero's death at the Battle of Wilson's Creek. Several histories of Connecticut fail to mention his name, while one disposes of him in a few lines. His sword and hat were turned over to the Connecticut Historical Society by the State of Connecticut on September 10, 1861, but the Society has no further record of them. The State erected a monument at his grave and maintains the area; the chimney of the house where he was born, with fireplaces restored, is used by picnickers and campers for outdoor cooking in Natchaug State Forest, which encompasses the site of the Lyon homestead. At the first town meeting in Eastford after the burial of General Lyon, it was "Voted to send bill to Connecticut Legislature for funeral expenses of General Lyon."

While his body lay in state in New York City, an unknown person

GENERAL NATHANIEL LYON'S MONUMENT

pinned the following inscription to the flag:

"To the Lion Hearted General Nathaniel Lyon

Thy name is immortal,
Thy battles are o'er;

Sleep, sleep, calmly sleep
On thy dear native shore."

General Nathaniel Lyon brought honor to the town of his birth; at least on the day of his funeral, Eastford was a place of renown.

"In these small inns [in Berkshire, Mass.], the disagreeable practice of rocking in the chair is seen in its excess. In the inn parlour are three or four rocking-chairs, in which sit ladies who are vibrating in different directions, and at various velocities, so as to try the head of a stranger almost as severely as the tobacco-chewer his stomach. How this lazy and ungraceful indulgence ever became general, I cannot imagine; but the nation seems so wedded to it, that I see little chance of its being forsaken. When American ladies come to live in Europe, they sometimes send home for a rocking-chair. A common wedding-present is a rocking-chair. A beloved pastor has every room in his house furnished with a rocking-chair by his grateful and devoted people. It is well that the gentlemen can be satisfied to sit still, or the world might be treated with the spectacle of the sublime American Senate in a new position; its fifty-two senators see-sawing in full deliberation, like the wise birds of a rookery in a breeze. If such a thing should ever happen, it will be time for them to leave off laughing at the Shaker worship."

Harriet Martineau,
Retrospect of Western Travel, I
(London, 1838), 72.

The "Spitting Lyon" of Vermont

by Charles W. McCollester

"It was the best of times; it was the worst of times . . . ," is the way the celebrated novel of the French Revolution, *A Tale of Two Cities*, begins. Charles Dickens' introductory paragraphs would apply equally well to the year 1798 in the infant republic of the United States of America.

Perceptive and pompous, incorruptible and waspish John Adams was President of the United States. The possibility of war with mighty revolutionary France darkened the international scene, while at home partisan politics and deep economic divisions created an apparently unbridgeable chasm between the weak and the powerful.

War with France did not come; the unbridgeable chasm was bridged; and the little nation, its deep divisions rendered bearable, turned its energies to building up rather than tearing down.

One man and one event—the man, at least, little noted once the danger was past—illustrate the crisis the emerging nation surmounted. To a degree, this man's life and the controversial events he engaged in have application today.

In the summer and fall of that fateful year of 1798, Congressman Matthew Lyon of Vermont became the first victim of the infamous Sedition Act just passed by Congress. Lyon's offense lay in writing and publishing remarks about President Adams he had already uttered in Congress. Citing those conditions under which he would support the Executive, Lyon concluded his letter: ". . . whenever I shall, on the part of the Executive, see every consideration of the public welfare swallowed up in a continual grasp for power, in an unbounded thirst for ridiculous pomp, foolish adulation, and selfish avarice . . . I shall not be their humble advocate."

Critical and perhaps unfair words, especially if one happened to be thin-skinned. But worthy of imprisonment? Why, then, was Matthew Lyon, the so-called "Spitting Lyon of Vermont," the one-time indentured servant risen to political and economic prominence—why was such a man singled out for prosecution?

There are many reasons, not the least of which was Lyon's sharp tongue, which stung even the most phlegmatic Federalists. Coupled with it was his quick Gaelic temper, illustrated by the spitting incident on the floor of Congress which earned him his nickname, and the subsequent rough-and-tumble fight in that same chamber which matched Lyon with the Honorable Roger Griswold, United States Representative from Connecticut.

The truth of the matter is that the Sedition Act, ill-conceived and hastily framed, represented an abortive attempt by the Federalist Party to solve the nation's domestic and foreign problems by muzzling its opposition, the clamorous, raucous, but rarely perfidious Republican dissidents.

Matthew Lyon deserves more than the footnote accorded him in most American history books. His ancestors in his native County Wicklow, Ireland, were landed gentry until the time of the first James. That monarch relieved the Irish of their land on the fraudulent excuse that the owners' titles were defective. The issue became personal in 1760 when Matthew, age ten, lost his father, slain in a protest against these evictions called the "White Boys" uprising.

The fact that he was left to fend for himself at so early an age undoubtedly contributed to the independent spirit that characterized Lyon in later years. By the age of twelve, he was working as an apprentice printer, his formal education—a smattering of classics and the usual English generalist training—already completed. Short, burly Matthew's early exposure to the world of commerce bestowed its benefits, not the least of which was friendship with another boy, Richard Brinsley Sheridan, later the parliamentary champion of India's teeming millions.

With prospects bleak in an Ireland that was nothing more than a British pawn, Matthew determined to seek his fortune in America. When he was fifteen he traded his liberty for sea passage, and the ship captain, influenced no doubt by the youngster's enterprising spirit as his cabin boy, auctioned Matthew off as an eighteen-year-old. For young Lyon this meant a three- instead of a six-year indenture.

A wealthy Litchfield, Connecticut, merchant, Jabez Bacon, bid for and obtained Matthew's services for three years for sixty dollars. Matthew respected and admired the shrewd Yankee trader's business acumen but differed sharply from his master in one vital respect: Bacon was a Tory conservative, Matthew a Whig.

Their differences were so vast that Matthew, with the aid of a nearby sympathetic Whig, paid up his three-year indenture at the end of a year. The friend supplied Matthew with two bulls, which he promptly sold to his master. The transaction not only meant freedom for Matthew; it gave him the oath that became his byword in later years: "By the bulls that redeemed me."

Litchfield proved a fortunate stopping-off place for Matthew Lyon. There he met Ethan Allen, for whom he worked, and Thomas Chittenden, later governor of Vermont for nineteen years. Both these men were to play major roles in shaping Matthew Lyon's future. Solid citizens of Litchfield though they were, they yearned for the unfettered life of the "frontier country" of Vermont. Lyon married Allen's niece in 1771; three years later he and Chittenden and their families followed Allen to Vermont.

Lyon halted on the western slopes of the Green Mountains, thirty miles east of Fort Ticonderoga, near the site of the present town of Wallingford. Once more it was a case of defying landholders pressing for eviction, only this time it was New Yorkers who claimed as their own the wild Green Mountains area that was part of the controverted New Hampshire Grants.

Lyon made his stand against eviction with the Green Mountain Boys, a group assembled and led by the redoubtable Ethan Allen. It was just three weeks after the first shots of the American Revolution had been fired at Concord and Lexington that the Green Mountain Boys, eighty-five strong, presented their impertinent demand for the surrender of Britain's fort at Ticonderoga "in the name of the Great Jehovah." More than forty years later Lyon estimated the plunder of cannon and military stores seized by the Green Mountain Boys as "worth more than a million dollars." As a moral boost, this first offensive action by the American rebels was worth uncounted millions more.

The Revolution was not one long glory road, however. An incident involving General Horatio Gates, the dubious "hero" of Saratoga, would haunt Lyon for years. When Lyon pulled back a small American holding unit before an advancing British army in northern Vermont, Gates had him cashiered from the service. While Lyon was soon reinstated and served the patriot cause with distinction, the allegation that he had been forced to wear a wooden sword, the symbol of cowardice, became a cruel political taunt that never failed to heat his Irish temper well beyond its boiling point.

By 1780 the penniless indentured servant of 1765 had already made his reputation in the rugged Vermont country. More was to come. Matthew Lyon would become a powerful politician in the state and national arenas; he would represent not one, but two—and, according to several reputable historians, three—states in the United States Congress; and he would compile a record of business achievements that—some observers claim—were at least a hundred years ahead of their time.

The launching of Lyon's business

career was accompanied by domestic tragedy. His wife, the mother of the first four Lyon children, died in 1782. The next year Matthew married Beulah Galusha, the widowed daughter of his old friend, Governor Thomas Chittenden. Nine children were born to this union. The year 1783 also saw Lyon purchase 1,000 acres near the headwaters of Lake Champlain and found the town of Fair Haven.

His first successful venture was a sawmill, and for his second, Lyon followed a biblical injunction: hauling debris from deserted battlefields at Ticonderoga, Crown Point, and Bennington, he literally turned swords into plowshares in his foundry. In 1784 he constructed a gristmill and, as a foretaste of things to come, purchased a printing press. Three years later he started an inn and in 1789 a leather tannery. Clearing the rich timber from the mountain slopes for his shipyards, Lyon even discovered and mined iron ore there. He turned the timber into prosperous commercial bottoms for the booming Lake Champlain-Montreal trade.

Possibly his greatest achievement in these busy years was his development of paper from the pulp of the basswood tree. Necessity mothered Lyon's discovery, as it has so many others, since the usual linen and cotton rag ingredients for papermaking were in short supply. Yet, necessity or not, the conversion of wood pulp to paper did not become a generally accepted process in the New World until over sixty years later.

Nor were Lyon's accomplishments limited to the practical arts. As a member of the Vermont General Assembly in 1791, he procured the enactment of a statute chartering the University of Vermont in Burlington.

Twenty years later, in Kentucky, Lyon repeated many of the Fair Haven successes. There too he discovered iron ore, mined it, and established an ironworks. There too he found basswood (though Kentuckians called it linden) and made use of the timber to build ships, only this time it went into gunboats for America in the War of 1812.

The man who in the halls of Congress a few years hence would be branded an "ignorant uncouth frontier demagogue" was by no means that in 1791, when he made his first bid for national political office. While able to hold his own in the turbulent Vermont border country, Lyon had married well, prospered in business, cemented powerful political ties, and was ready at age forty-one for the "main chance."

All his efforts at nationwide recognition were frustrated until 1797, when Lyon became one of the few Democratic-Republicans from New England elected to the United States House of Representatives. He could never be accused of timidity; true to form, it did not take him long to make his presence felt in Philadelphia. He shared the frontiersman's natural loathing for royalist pretensions, and when he found the Federalist-dominated Congress practically prostrating itself at the feet of President John Adams, it was more than he could bear.

A custom of "waiting on" the President to learn when and where that august personage would receive an address by the new Congress was already established by 1798. Lyon made his impatience with "courtly customs" and his faith in democracy unmistakably clear to his fellow Congressmen:

I cannot say, it is true, that I am descended from the bastards of Oliver Cromwell, or his courtiers, or from the Puritans who punished their horses for breaking the Sabbath, or from those who persecuted the Quakers or hanged the witches. I can, however, say that this is my country, because I have no other; and I own a share of it which I have bought by means of honest industry; I have fought for my country. In every day of her trouble I have repaired to her standard and have conquered under it. Conquest has led my country to independence, and, being independent, I call no man's blood in question.

Such sentiments did not set well with the patrician New England Federalists. A more serious failing of Lyon, in their eyes, was his growing stature among Democratic-Republicans. The worst of these gadflies criticized all things Federalist, from the President's person to his foreign policy to the party's alleged evil influence on the weather. Lyon was all too close to Mr. Jefferson, the Vice-President, and he shared with that gentleman views on revolutionary France that, in Federalist eyes, verged on the treasonable.

On the floor of Congress one day early in 1798, Lyon was chatting with colleagues about what he described as the peculiar backwardness of the people of Connecticut. The words, intended for the ears of Representative Roger Griswold and others nearby, singled out the "malign influence of Connecticut politicians." When Lyon boasted that if he were to seek office in Connecticut the voters there would gladly elect him to replace their present worthless representatives, Griswold could stand no more.

"When you come to Connecticut, Mr. Lyon, I trust you will wear your wooden sword," he jeered. (Lyon's supposed cowardice during the Revolution was common knowledge now, trumpted far and wide by the pen of William Cobbett in *Porcupine's Gazette*.)

Lyon had cast the bait, but he was likewise the first to seize it. He turned and spat full in the face of Roger Griswold.

Some two weeks later, again on the floor of Congress, Griswold seized the opportunity to avenge this insult. He attacked Lyon with a cane, while Lyon fought back with a pair of fire tongs, barely missing his adversary's head with one vicious swipe.

The Federalists advocated expelling both combatants, though their most trenchant barbs were naturally reserved for the Vermont Republican, who, besides being a "spitting animal" and "depraved," was an Irishman. Harrison Gray Otis wrote: "I feel grieved that the saliva of an Irishman should be left upon the face of an American, and he, a New England man."

For fourteen days Congress debated the question of Lyon's expulsion. Congressman Dana of Massachusetts described Lyon as a "kennel of filth." The fastidious Otis commented that even a brothel would not tolerate such conduct. The ouster move failed, however, when the Federalists could not muster the necessary two-thirds majority.

Matthew Lyon kept his saliva in his mouth for the balance of the session, but he missed few opportunities to tongue lash the "warmonger" Federalists. When the Sedition Act was passed on July 4, 1798, it was plain to everyone that Lyon was its prime Congressional target. Besides publishing the so-called "attack" on President Adams (which, incidentally, was written and submitted, though not published, before the Sedition Act's passage), he permitted the printing of a letter from Joel Barlow, then in France, which urged Congress to commit the President to

a madhouse. In his own journal bearing the mouthfilling title, *Lyon's Republican Magazine, the Scourge of Aristocracy and Repository of Important Political Truths,* Lyon advised Americans that they should prepare to resist Federalist efforts to impose a "state of abject slavery."

Lyon posted the "Adams letter" to the *Vermont Journal* in Windsor on June 20, more than three weeks before the Sedition Act took effect; but it was no inted until well after July 14. The letter was a flimsy, shaky peg on which to hang a sedition indictment, but that fact did not deter the eager government forces.

The indictment, served on October 5, contained three counts: the "scandalous and seditious" letter published in the Journal; the "libeling of President Adams and the Senate" by publishing the Joel Barlow letter; and "aiding and abetting" the publication of this second letter.

Lyon based his defense on constitutional law. He asserted that the court had no jurisdiction because the Sedition Act was unconstitutional; moreover, he had written the letter before the law was passed; his writings had no "bad intent"; finally—and most galling of all to his political foes—the contents of the letter were true.

Associate Justice Samuel Paterson of the United States Supreme Court, who presided at the trial because it was held in his Rutland, Vermont, jurisdiction, demolished the defense points contemptuously. He told the jury in plain terms that the Act's constitutionality was not for them to decide. Rather, they should weigh whether Lyon did, in fact, publish the writings as alleged, and if so, whether he had published them "seditiously," that is, with evil intent.

It did not take the jury long to decide the "Spitting Lyon's" fate. Guilty as charged, the jurymen said. In meting out the sentence of a $1,000 fine and four months' imprisonment, Justice Paterson lamented that the Sedition Act did not permit him to inflict as heavy a punishment as the common law allowed.

Immediately after sentencing, Lyon was caged in a filthy cell in Vergennes. The "vile career of the beast of the mountain was ended," his enemies rejoiced. But while Lyon had to endure the company of horse thieves and counterfeiters, the baiting of a vindictive jailer, and the cold of an unheated cell during a typical Vermont winter, he could still write. And all the Republican newspapers in the country published his letters. In one, to Senator Stevens Mason of Virginia, Lyon declared, "It is quite a new kind of jargon to call a Representative of the People an Opposer of the Government, because he does not, as a Legislator, advocate and acquiesce in every proposition that comes from the Executive."

The jubilation of Lyon's Federalist foes proved premature. In the September 1798 election "ragged Matt, the Democrat" had come within twenty-six votes of a clear majority over five contenders. In the December runoff, although still in jail, he was re-elected to Congress by an overwhelming 2,000 votes.

There are conflicting versions of how Lyon's fine and court costs ($1,060.96 in all) were paid. It is certain, at least, that there was no lack of donors ready to make the payment when the jail doors swung open in February 1799. The venerable Senator Mason was there with $1,000 he had carried in his saddlebags all the way from the Old Dominion. Similarly prepared were a rich Vermont friend of Lyon, Apollos Austin (later the first settler of Austin, Texas), and Lyon's faithful wife, Beulah.

The "never-say-die" Federalists had a new indictment ready to present Lyon as he left the jail. But briskly brushing aside the process-server, Lyon jumped into the sleigh beside his wife and cried, "I'm on my way to Congress."

Lyon proceeded in triumph to Philadelphia. Fellow Republicans there feted him at a party where, as William Cobbett put it, everyone got as "drunk as democrats generally do whenever they get a chance to swig."

Congressional Federalists at once renewed their efforts to expel Lyon. While ostensibly concerned about the sedition issue, their real worry was the election of 1800, which they were reasonably sure would be thrown into Congress. There was little Lyon's foes would not do to insure another Federalist vote from Vermont. The effort failed once again, and Lyon was able to cast an important vote for Thomas Jefferson when the electoral college tie between Jefferson and Aaron Burr threw the decision into the House of Representatives.

How decisive was the Lyon vote for Jefferson in February 1801? Historians dispute its importance and differ in their assessment of the motivations of those Congressmen whose changed votes were also crucial in Jefferson's election. The followers of the defeated John Adams voted for Burr in the early balloting solely to prevent that archpriest of Republicanism, Thomas Jefferson, from attaining the Presidency. Since the voting was by states and since Vermont, Kentucky, and Tennessee had now joined the original thirteen, a majority of nine states must vote for either of the contestants in order to effect his election.

The delegations from eight states supported Jefferson, six backed Burr, and two—Vermont and Maryland—were evenly divided and thus were forced to cast blank ballots. Vermont's two Congressmen, Lyon and Lewis Morris, canceled each other out through thirty-five long ballots; Maryland was in a similar situation, two of its Congressmen

backing Burr and two Jefferson. On the thirty-sixth ballot, after six days and nights of wrangling, Congressman Morris of Vermont was absent. Lyon then cast Vermont's "decisive" ninth vote for Jefferson.

The question of decisiveness arises from the fact that on the same thirty-sixth ballot Delaware's one-man delegation, Federalist James A. Bayard, along with the Maryland group, did not vote. Thus, barring a major switch by pro-Jefferson states, any chance of Burr's election was already rendered impossible. Why Morris was absent can also be conjectured about. Whether it might have been the result of pressure exerted by the moderate Hamiltonian wing of the Federalists is not certain. What is certain is that Congressman Matthew Lyon, only two years out of jail, provided Thomas Jefferson with the vote he needed to become President of the United States.

That same year 1801 Lyon moved to Eddyville, Kentucky, and by 1803 was back in Congress as a Representative from his new state. During this later eight-year tenure, Lyon matured remarkably. With a vision far ahead of his time, he repeatedly denounced some of the tyrannical rules then prevailing in the House of Representatives. The dictatorial power of the Speaker in appointing committees, the growing tendency of the national government to centralize, the nomination of Presidential candidates by a small group of politicians meeting in secret caucus—all these practices inflamed the eloquent Lyon. And he did not hesitate to speak his mind.

He was the same old colorful Lyon in other ways. He was the first Congressman able to hold his own in debate with silver-tongued John Randolph of Virginia; he declaimed, Cassandra-like, about the inherent evils of President Madison's Embargo. And in 1814, then out of Congress three years, he made his power felt by publicly castigating the Hartford Convention which, if successful, would have severed New England from the Union. On the personal level, too, he offered counsel in this controversy, advising his old Massachusetts friend, Josiah Quincy, that secession was not the answer to the sectional rifts brought on by the War of 1812.

A decade earlier, Lyon's watchdog instincts had been aroused by the Aaron Burr "conspiracy," an alleged plot to establish an empire in the Louisiana Purchase lands. Lyon's wise admonitions were instrumental in preventing the innocent involvement (and subsequent disgrace) of his distinguished colleagues, Andrew Jackson and Henry Clay.

In many ways the Eddyville of Lyon's later years resembled the Fair Haven of his early ones. His shipbuilding operation on the Cumberland River boomed for a time, but the flotilla of gunboats he built for the government in the War of 1812 was destroyed in a storm, and he lost a fortune. His Eddyville ironworks are memorable, too, particularly for their pioneering in the use of fluorite, a metal producing superior fusion in iron connections.

In these declining years, Lyon's financial troubles increased. To bail his seventy-year-old friend out of his difficulties, President James Monroe, in 1820, appointed Lyon United States Factor to the Cherokee Nation in the Arkansas Territory. There is a dispute among historians as to whether Lyon was elected as Arkansas' delegate to Congress in 1821. One quite reliable historian says Lyon won election on his second try, but died August 1, 1822, at Spadra Bluff, Arkansas, before he could take his seat. Another writer, usually more laudatory, reports that Lyon failed in both his 1819 and 1821 campaigns, though he implies that political chicanery caused his downfall the second time.

Whether Matthew Lyon represented three or two states in Congress is unimportant now. Whether his accomplishments as founder and "grand seigneur" of two flourishing early American towns were unique —that, too, no longer matters. His contributions as an industrialist and entrepreneur have withstood the test of time, though like all other "firsts" in the world of commerce they have been superseded. What does matter is that Lyon was that rare rugged individualist who balances an independent spirit with the sobering realization that he owes much to his fellow man.

It is significant that Lyon should represent the backwood mountains of Vermont, the "seedbed of democrats" in Kentucky, and, possibly, the cotton-growing "kingdom" of Arkansas. In his career he typified both the northern frontiersman and the "men of the Western waters," legends destined for honored niches in American folklore.

Matthew Lyon personifies much that was best in the America of the early nineteenth century. It might not be such a bad prescription for the late twentieth, either.

WARNING

"This is to give due Notice to all Owners of HENS in my Neighborhood that I have this Day bought Half a Pound of Powder, and Shot in Proportion; and having fixed a new Flint in my old Militia Gun, am determined to fire upon, and endeavour to kill, all FOWLS that may appear in my Garden, from and after Three oClock in the Afternoon of Monday next, until the first Day of October; and deeming this Determination not inconsistent with the Principles of good Neighborhood, if any Person should look *cross* at me on this Account, I am likewise determined not to care for that.

An Up-Town Man,
who owns
a small Garden.

N.B. Colonel Whipple has more Powder to sell."

Providence Gazette, 9 Apr. 1796.

General Tom Thumb

by Katherine Saunders

In November 1842, P. T. Barnum, the great showman, stopped at the Franklin Hotel in Bridgeport, Connecticut. There he heard talk of a dwarf who played daily in the streets and was a great curiosity to the city crowds. The child was incredibly small, only two feet one inch in height, and weighed fifteen pounds, smaller than the average three-year-old. He was pink-cheeked and healthy, well proportioned and charming. He had blonde hair and dark intelligent eyes.

With his natural astuteness, Barnum realized immediately, that here was a priceless attraction for his American Museum, as he called his theatre in New York.

He immediately visited the boy's parents, Mr. and Mrs. Sherwood Stratton. The boy was Charles. With Barnum's genius for showmanship, he immediately began teaching the boy jokes and impersonations. Charles took to the stage like a swan to water, and an exciting life opened.

Barnum had no trouble convincing Mrs. Stratton she should bring her small son to New York, and on Thanksgiving Day of 1842 they arrived. It is a question which was the more thankful, Barnum or Mrs. Stratton. It was somewhat puzzling to her to find Charles advertised as General Tom Thumb, a dwarf *eleven* years old, just arrived from England. Charles was six.

But Barnum knew people in this country valued an import far more highly than a domestic product. The "General Tom Thumb" was pure inspiration.

Tom Thumb kept his mother and father with him. Barnum paid the munificent salary of twenty-five dollars a week plus a tutor and all expenses. But the tremendous publicity he gave the boy at his "Museum" in New York built up public interest so high that at one time it was estimated 80,000 people came to see him before he left for England. Dressed in smart little costumes, he sang, danced, and was a sensation. The New York *Evening Post* of January 16, 1844 reported, "General Tom Thumb has engaged passage to England but may be seen at three, seven, and nine as the packet will not sail today on account of easterly winds prevailing!"

P. T. Barnum. *Reproduced from the collections of the Library of Congress.*

It took nineteen days to get to England. There Barnum was as homesick as Tom Thumb and is said to have sat down and cried. It was a strange country and he was scared.

But almost immediately the proprietor of the Waxworks called and wanted to put an image of the midget in his collection. This was in Liverpool, where Barnum soon had an offer to exhibit his little friend at tuppence a head. He declared that this was not enough, since he never had received less than twenty-five cents. The great showman was nothing if not courageous and decided he would proceed immediately to London and visit the Queen.

Prince Albert's father had just died and the court was in mourning, but Maddox of the Princess Theatre invited them for three appearances which large crowds attended. That was all Barnum would allow; he had much larger ideas in mind.

They rented Lord Talbot's mansion on Grafton Street and lived in style, sending out invitations to royalty.

Her Majesty the Queen was titillated by rumors of this fabulous little creature and no doubt restrained her curiosity with difficulty.

Horace Greeley, good friend of Barnum, had given him letters to newspaper people and to the American minister to the Court of St. James. In this way, in spite of the court's being in mourning, Barnum met Queen Victoria.

The Baroness Rothschild sent her carriage for Tom Thumb and his guardian and they were tenderly brought before the Queen. All the lords and ladies were sitting on golden chairs, and General Tom Thumb strutted down the hall to her Majesty, trilling "Good evening, ladies and gentlemen." Victoria took his little hand and led him around the picture gallery, which he pronounced "first-rate." Tom Thumb sang and danced for the company, upon which he was given a standing ovation.

It came time for the assembly to back out, not to turn their backs in the presence of the Queen. Barnum, six feet two and Tom Thumb, two feet one, were amusing to see, and the company laughed even more when Tom had to turn and run a few steps to keep up with the others.

Their laughter didn't hurt his feelings, since he loved to clown.

Barnum had a sumptuous little coach built for the child in England. It was twenty inches high and eleven wide, painted blue with red and white wheels. The upholstery was velvet. Two Shetland ponies drew him, and small boys acted as coachman and footman, wearing blue velvet coats with silver lace, red velvet breeches, cocked hats, and wigs. Barnum never did things by halves.

King Louis Philippe of France now invited, in fact commanded, them to appear in the Tuilleries. Barnum dared to ask if General Tom Thumb's carriage might not appear in the avenue reserved for royalty for fear it might be crushed in the Paris crowd. The King graciously permitted this, and thousands cheered "Le General Tom Pouce."

Tickets were sold for the Salle Musard, whereby 5,500 francs were added to Barnum's fortune. Seats had to be reserved two months in advance.

When the General returned to Egyptian Hall in London, the historical painter Benjamin Robert Haydon wrote, "They rush by the thousands to see Tom Thumb. They push; they fight; they scream; they faint. But they rush by my paintings and don't see them." This was the man to whom Wordsworth sent his poems "piping hot from the brain." Haydon's exhibit brought in seven-

Tom Thumb and his wife. *Reproduced from the collections of the Library of Congress.*

teen pounds and Tom Thumb's 600 in one day. The artist committed suicide. Barnum had grown so rich he tried without success to buy Shakespeare's home and Mme Tussaud's famous waxworks.

Barnum took Tom Thumb's father into partnership with him; the receipts from Europe alone were said to be 150,000 pounds sterling.

The little General after he grew up was a very religious person; a letter to a clergyman friend states, "I have traveled fifty thousand miles, been before more crown heads than any Yankee living except my friend, P. T. Barnum, been kissed by Queens of England, France, Belgium and Spain. I read my Bible every day and love my Creator. He has given me a small body but I

Tom Thumb, Miss Warren, Commodore Nutt, and Barnum. *Photo by Brady, reproduced from the collections of the Library of Congress.*

Mrs. Tom Thumb. *Reproduced from the collections of the Library of Congress.*

believe He has not contracted my brain nor soul."

Commodore Nutt, a seventeen-year-old dwarf, handsome and slightly taller than Tom Thumb, and Lavinia Warren, a lovely little lady who had gone to public schools and actually had become a teacher in Middleboro, Massachusetts, were added to the show.

The Commodore was a gay young rake. General Tom Thumb, now a rich man, owned a yacht, a miniature mansion built by his father, and a string of ponies. Both these tiny men fell in love with Lavinia and at one time they got into a fight, during which Mr. Nutt knocked down Mr. Thumb!

Barnum, who looked after his company as though they were children, invited Tom Thumb to his own home in Bridgeport, Connecticut, to give him a chance to propose. The Commodore arrived just at the crucial moment when the General was asking if he might accompany Lavinia as her husband when the show returned to Europe. The little Commodore wished them happiness, turned on his heel, and left.

Tom Thumb and Lavinia were married at Grace Church, New York City, on February 10, 1863. The General was then twenty-five and his bride twenty-two. President Lincoln sent as a wedding gift a lovely set of fire screens, Mrs. Cornelius Vanderbilt a coral and gold brooch and earrings. The governors of all the

83

Barnum's Bridgeport home, litho. by Sarony & Major. *Reproduced from the collections of the Library of Congress.*

nearby states attended. Two thousand invitations were sent to notables, all of whom accepted. The Bishop almost consented to officiate but didn't quite dare.

In the course of their honeymoon the couple visited President and Mrs. Lincoln who entertained them.

General Tom Thumb in addition to his yacht and string of ponies now possessed a fortune in precious stones. He looked like a business man, smoked cigars, became a third degree mason. He and his wife tried living in seclusion for a time but were miserable and returned immediately to show business. They toured Europe with other famous dwarfs including Commodore Nutt, Lavinia's dwarf sister, Minnie, and General Grant, Jr., who married Minnie in 1878. Neighbors in Middleboro, where the Grants lived, saw Minnie cutting out infinitesimal baby clothes, one-sixth the normal size, from doll clothes patterns. But

poor Minnie didn't live through childbirth. She and her baby died.

Before this, in 1865, the whole dwarf company toured the world, visiting Queen Victoria for the second time, Napoleon III and the Empress Eugenie, Pius IX, Victor Emmanuel of Italy, and William I of Germany, this time on their own, not under Barnum's auspices. But Barnum, prone to go bankrupt at times because of his grandiose undertakings, was at one time put back on his feet by the minute people whom he had befriended and made rich.

General Tom Thumb died in 1883 at age forty-five and was buried with Masonic honors. He had spent too much on his yachts and horses; consequently his wife, who married again, had to run a general store in Middleboro, "Primo's Pastime."

A collection of the royal gifts and some of the small furniture still exists in Middleboro.

The General's Daughter

by Bernard Quinn

On a bitter cold and bright March night in 1778 a prosperous but rather troubled Massachusetts farmer stepped from the warmth and comfort of Cooley's Inn in the center of the settlement called Brookfield Township, and braced himself for the trudge to his home and family, a mile and more distant. Winding the long wool muffler snug around his throat, Joshua Spooner headed out of the village at a pace belying his forty-seven years, with head well down against the biting wind that also cut to the bone. His heavy boots clumped as he made his way carefully along the frozen cart path, checking for icy patches by the brightness of an almost full moon bathing the light snowfall which had come just at the supper hour.

The journey that lay before Spooner was one he had managed many times, on foot, on horseback, or in a jouncing farm cart. His stride was brisk. It was no night to loiter, particularly when one's wife waited by the hearth, the children slept, and the bells in the meeting-house at Casey's Crossroads already had tolled nine. Besides, there was war about, and times were troubled. It was the cruel winter of Valley Forge, and there was uneasiness in the countryside, particularly after dusk when questionable characters spawned by the war were often about.

The husky farmer picked his way with care over the ankle-deep layer of snow lest he slip and lie there the night—and suffer unto death in the cold with injury, for no soul of good heart likely would pass along the cart-path through the lonely hours before daybreak.

At that same hour Joshua's wife, Bathsheba, was tidying up her kitchen in the small farmhouse to the west. She had looked in on the sleeping children in the chilly and raftered room adjoining. Occasionally she stopped by the tiny window near the door, peering at the whiteness that lay before the door and across the fields. She was certain her husband had by then left the inn where—as he had told her—he had business. The clock showed well past nine, so all was well. He had mentioned he would sup at Cooley's and would head for the hearth at nine. If Joshua was nothing else he was punctual—an attribute she would cherish this night. He could just be passing the long low stonewall stretching between the wooded patches where he had been felling trees for a fortnight. He might even be near the old Indian well where the Quabaugs stopped so often when on hunting or fishing parties between the Quabaug river and the Winnimessitt, an area where deer, ducks, and trout abounded.

Joshua clumped along, noting ahead the sudden flitting form that meant a fox. It crossed the cart-path like a feather in a wind, and melted into the night that was its domain. The farmer felt the pangs that gnawed within him—he was one of few words, and what crowded his thoughts was not that which one could discuss with other villagers on the rare occasions they were encountered. He could only suffer within himself and wonder.

He and the fox were not the only ones stirring about that night—but only the fox was privy to that. The flitting form the homeward-bound traveler had seen was skirting along a slight rise overlooking the cart-path, scenting for whatever other life might be about—troublesome man or other life. Suddenly the sly forager caught a scent, paused, checked, and then sprang away, quickly leaving be-

hind whatever had alarmed him. It was not Joshua Spooner's odor that he had pulled from the frosty air; rather it was the pervasive smells from figures huddled snug behind the stonewall, near a clearing and not far from the barway. Suddenly alerted, the lone hunter doubled back along its tracks and trotted into the nearby frozen-over swamp. Spooner continued on, unaware an alarm had been sounded and it was he who stood in danger. Home and warmth—if nothing more—were not far, and hot tea with rum would make the trek in the cold worth the discomfort.

Unknown to the worried farmer, three men lay in wait between him and his wife and the young Spooners. The trio were bent on murder—an action they were certain they would complete and which they would have to accomplish to collect the rewards they had been promised. There was blackness in their hearts, and with eagerness they looked forward to their mission; with care they had selected the spot where they would do violence—it was but a few strides from the makeshift barway through which Joshua would be dragged to the deep and frozen well at the edge of the growth of young birches bright in the moon showing through their branches.

Each was drawn to the other through another common denominator—they were army deserters; two were from the armies of the Colonies, then fighting through the third winter of a hard war that would extend into the next decade. Their partner in wickedness was from the invading redcoat army of King George III, and specifically from one of General "Gentleman Johnny" Burgoyne's units.

In the frosty stillness the three heard the sound of someone's booted strides approaching; with patience they waited. Yes, it was Spooner, whom each had seen so often. Let him come astride the barway, they agreed. Their prey was a big man and strong—but it was he against three. The assassins completed their grisly task without mishap or delay, and well before midnight the man who had supped at Cooley's on barley broth, bread, and salt beef lay crumpled, bludgeoned, and lifeless deep in the Indian well, by then long with a floor of ice. The killers had carried Spooner there after his brief stand against a club, muscle, and knives.

Within the hour the murderous deserters sat by a heavy oaken table, accepting in turn the payments promised. The paymaster, who believed their accounts of what had transpired near the barway, doled out their rewards—making certain there was also rum for all, and plenty. There was laughter there, interspersed with ribald remarks, and had one been passing by the lonely farmhouse there might be envy of the sounds from behind the tiny window with the dull light.

The paymaster was Bathsheba Spooner, suddenly an attractive widow of thirty-two years—the mother of the children sleeping soundly beside the raucous exchanges filling the candle-lit kitchen. So certain was the brown-haired conspirator that her accomplices would not fail her in fulfilling their part of the agreement that, true to her word, she had already collected clothing and her late husband's other effects that were about, and what money she could lay hand to—for the sharing. So it was that the daughter of a General in Washington's army paid her guests as promised—a promise made a few evenings earlier as she had entertained her visitors.

The three guests participating in that macabre hour of reward, when their wages for the deed were paid them by the woman who had proposed that they do her husband to death, were by name Ezra Ross, William Brooks, and James Buchanan. Ross and Brooks had deserted the American forces during the darkest hours of the Colonies' struggle for freedom; Buchanan had deserted from Burgoyne's troops after the British commander was roundly whipped at the Battle of Saratoga in 1777.

Joshua Spooner's personal effects were divided and accepted. Time was to reveal that Ross and Brooks left and went their way. To Buchanan there was greater reward offered and accepted. He stopped the night, enjoying the Spooner bed and board. It was the lad from Lancashire, according to subsequent testimony from villagers, who was the darling of Bathsheba during the weeks he had visited the Spooner homestead alone or in company with his mates. The swaggering tough had been presented the husband's favorite watch—proof that he was held in high esteem by the new widow. There is no record of how the three deserters fell in together, but later it was learned that they originally were invited to the doomed farmer's home by Bathsheba herself.

Bathsheba (she of the Biblical name derived from the beautiful woman who, in the tenth century B.C., became King David's wife after he—in his lusting after Sheba's daughter—had sent her first husband Uriah to his death) was the daughter of Timothy Ruggles of Hardwick. Her father, graduated from Harvard College in 1732, was serving under General Washington at the time of the crime, and an historical accounting of General Ruggles states: "He was one of the most prominent citizens of Massachusetts, and indeed of New England, in both military and civil affairs."

It was not long before villagers noticed the boisterous and unwelcome trio, carousing and showing signs of wealth in their midst. Beyond that, the strangers who had in earlier days in the area been somewhat furtive in their movements, now brazenly were wearing among them a coat, boots, a belt, and other apparel known to be Joshua Spooner's—all knew the townsman and that which was his. When Buchanan flaunted the favorite watch there were questions upon questions, mutterings and whispered discussion in candlelight at tables in Cooley's place. After all, Spooner had not been seen at his farm or in the village for a time. Some whispered a horrible rumor, and it became more pressing with time's passage to seek out the truth. There were those in the Township who were aware Joshua was upset with his wife for inviting strangers into their household, hosting them, and particularly in wartime, and when one of them had served with the enemy among his Majesty's forces.

Eventually the widow and her consorts were rounded up, jailed by the township's two constables, and questioned regarding the whereabouts of the man whose absence had become a topic of concern even within neighboring settlements. The truth was soon found out, and the frozen remains were drawn from the Indian well. Accounts of events by each of the quartet were noted by the authorities, and soon the deserters were under the charge of murder, Bathsheba under that of complicity to murder.

Exposure of the crime—and the wife's involvement to the hilt—created a sensation throughout Massachusetts, and news of it reached also to far places. The case was tried at the April term of the County Court of Worcester, with the Honorable Robert T. Paine as State's Attorney, and the Honorable Levi Lincoln as counsel for the defendants. The facts concerning all aspects of the crime were admitted by the principals, to the horror of the court and the public. What a meeting of minds spectators noted—three army deserters and a General's daughter!

Counsel Lincoln's principal stand in his defense of Mrs. Spooner was that she was a person of "unsound or distracted mind." In centering his efforts on saving the widow from the gallows, he extended little intercession on behalf of the three killers, and charged there was error in the court's complete disregard of his defense that Bathsheba was not of sound mind. Her conduct before the crime, to which some villagers were privy, had convinced them and those with whom they gossiped, that she was mentally unstable. Despite all efforts she stood charged as a murderer. The Hardwick town history commented:

The conduct of Mrs. Spooner, both be-fore and after the murder, bears evident marks of insanity. It appeared at the trial that these strangers had been invited into her house and had been entertained, during which time she engaged them to kill her husband . . . She not only rewarded the murderers with money but dressed them in her husband's clothes.

Bathsheba's defense counsel presented a stirring plea for his client:

The whole evidence was that of a fool or a distracted person. Born in high rank of life, well educated and accomplished, a wife and a mother, and in the enjoyment of good estate, what object would she have in undertaking such a detestable crime? . . . . Whom did she trust with the management of such a villainy that so affected her reputation, her safety, her life, her children and others? The answer was to Tories, regulars, deserters, strangers and foreigners . . . . After the murder she gives the murderers his watch, his buckles, waistcoat, breeches, shirts, and even has them put the items on, to be worn in the eyes of the world, where they were well known to be Spooner's clothes . . . . Was this the conduct of a person in the exercise of reason? Would it have been less rational to have written on their foreheads, in capitals, 'The murderers of Mister Spooner!'

Counsel Lincoln's pleading to the jury was of no avail—the verdict for Bathsheba, as for the others, was "guilty." They were sentenced to be executed at Worcester, the county seat, on June 4th. The Court Council did grant, out of hand, a one month respite—a development which would lend to the entire bizarre affair a twist which would have repercussions of consequence a month later, and raise the haunting question as to whether more lives were taken in expiation than the court had directed, based on the "guilty" findings.

The one-month respite in execution of sentence came about through the efforts of the Reverend Thaddeus MacCarthy of Worcester, who had provided religious ministration for the doomed widow. MacCarthy had come upon information he felt it was his duty to report to the court, to wit: ". . . The unhappy woman declares that she is several months advanced in her pregnancy." The court then arranged for a group of midwives to ascertain if there were grounds for the claim by the "unhappy woman"—one submitted to the Court by a man of the cloth. The midwives, together with some assisting matrons, informed the Court the widow's claim was without substantiation.

The new date set for the hangings was July 2nd, and it was a banner one for citizens crowded on the common of Worcester—they were treated to four hangings that afternoon, and news accounts of the "spectacle" noted there was a tremendous gathering on hand.

Bathsheba's father, his career ruined and despondent in mind, journeyed to far off Nova Scotia well before his daughter's end, there to settle a new home and await the coming of Mrs. Ruggles, who had remained in Hardwick until after the day in Worcester.

An examination by authorities of Bathsheba's remains proved she indeed had been pregnant—the midwives and matrons had erred! The error fathered the frightening question: had Massachusetts taken two lives in its killing of the screaming woman, struggling against her death in a drenching rain?

One happenstance darkening the hangman's hour was the vicious rainstorm which swept over the scene. A Worcester newspaper account of the events reports:

Just before they reached the gallows, one of the most terrific thunderstorms came up, and darkened the heavens, and all together conspired to produce a scene of most dreadful terror in the minds of the throng of 5,000 people, assembled to witness the spectacle.

New Hampshire School Days in the 1860's

by Mary-Maud Oliver

The founders of New England and their successors have ever been seriously committed to the "business" of education. The report to the State of New Hampshire Department of Common Schools in 1858–59 stated that although the schools were improving constantly and there was a great interest in education among the people, too little financial support was being provided:

Individuals and states disburse their revenues for the advance of commerce and trade and the improvements of all perishable agencies of a material prosperity with a liberal hand while they dole out with a narrow economy under checks and guards, the pittances of a public support given to the schools, the true source of our prosperity and the ultimate refuge of the defense of liberty.

In 1861–62, Mr. H. Merrill, reporting for the School Commission of Merrimac County, warned that in spite of the just demands of the "national perils and duties" the common school must not be neglected. The schools of the county were giving sound training in reading, spelling, and arithmetic, but he was emphatic in his conviction that these subjects were best taught in the "old method by which our fathers and mothers acquired good and sound discipline. To attain a well-trained mind and a habit of close, accurate thinking is the end of discipline in the schoolroom."

He commended the schools of Concord and its districts because out of the thirty-four teachers in the twenty-three schools, all but seven had continued throughout the year and in most cases were "good" teachers. The salaries listed for these "good" teachers amounted to $33.52 for males and $15.18 for females.

That New England educators felt responsible for the future welfare of the country is evident in this challenging report:

Intelligent men and women are the great staple of New England. We cannot compete successfully with the west in agriculture nor the middle states in commerce. But, happily, if we cherish our system of education and give vigorous support, then, on the margin of the

Republic we may hope to continue in the future as in the past, the center of its mental and intellectual life. The common schools are the peoples' colleges.

This report ended with a solemn warning:

there is a constant drain upon New England of youthful vigor and intelligence in its ceaseless tide of emigration. It is our business to educate those who found new states and mold society. Herein is an exalted privilege and fearful responsibility.

One of the thousands of families who were a part of "this ceaseless tide of emigration" was that of Florence Cushman Milner. She was born in Greensboro, Vermont, in the year 1855, but the family soon moved to Concord, New Hampshire, where her father was employed by the Abbott-Downing Carriage Company.

It was in Concord that she received her primary education from the age of four and a half to ten. This training, she often remarked later, was an excellent one, in spite of its oldfashioned methods. During her forty-four years of teaching she was frequently asked how she had acquired her method of instruction, since she had begun her career when she was sixteen, the year she graduated from high school. Her answer was that as far as she could remember her methods were those used to explain problems to her when a child in Concord.

Florence Milner as a young girl. *Photo courtesy of the author.*

That she was an eminently successful and long-remembered teacher is proved both by the numerous letters she received, all during her life, from former pupils giving her credit for their achievements and by the many articles published by and about her.

In 1916 she returned joyfully to her native New England to assume charge of the then new Farnsworth Room in Widener Library where she remained until her retirement in 1937. She continued to live in Cambridge in close contact with the University community and often visited by her former students. On her ninetieth birthday in 1945 she received one-hundred and fifty letters and one hundred roses from her "boys and girls" of the Grand Rapids, Michigan, high school of the 1890's.

Her enthusiasm for and interest in education from the earliest years

92

The Call house at far left, where Florence Milner lived as a child. *Photo courtesy of the New Hampshire Historical Society.*

through college and adult life never waned, so it was only natural that during her years of retirement she began to write her remembrances of the Concord school. After eighty years she still remembered the teachers and the school as being excellent for the "training of the mind and the formation of character."

NEW HAMPSHIRE SCHOOL DAYS IN THE EIGHTEEN SIXTIES

by Florence Milner

When I was four and a half, my conscious, systematic education began. Ella, my constant playmate had reached her educational majority and was to start school in the spring. The rules were stretched to allow me to enter with her. Since our little white cottage was just across the street from the State House in Concord, New Hampshire, and the school building was only across the Unitarian Church Yard, my journey

to and from school could be watched from my mother's room. There were no kindergartens then, so we were put at once into the first primary, but at that time no one seemed afraid that my nature or my intellect would be warped by entering school so early.

Before this time, I had "picked up," by what might now be called the natural method, a bit of education. On the hearth of the kitchen stove, the name of its maker and the place of its manufacture stood out in relief. By tagging my mother around and asking her over and over again what this or that letter was, I learned most of the alphabet. The name of the stove, I learned later, was "Tilden's Improved—Barre, Vermont." Having mastered its fourteen different letters, the others were discovered from a set of blocks. Next came spelling out words from a primer. According to modern methods, that was all wrong but my mother didn't know that. I always pronounced "the" with full value to the long "e" and I read "I see *the* cat," with a triumphant jump at the cat. In spite of these unscientific methods, I could read my primer fairly well before I started off to school.

On that eventful first day, the child that was I wore a pink and white gingham tire, as the all-covering apron was called, white stockings, and patent leather ankle-ties with straps buttoning across the instep.

After many a painful tug of the comb, the mass of yellow hair was reduced to smooth curls that hung to the waist. Over them went a white shaker, one instrument of torture the inquisition missed. Picture a long cylinder of stiffly varnished straw, open at one end. There was a place cut out for the neck so that the head could be driven far back into the cavern. A long gingham cape gathered around the cut-out part hung down over the shoulders and excluded all cooling breezes. Strings tied in a prim bow held the abominable structure in place, pressing hair about the neck, making hearing impossible, breathing difficult, and seeing equally so, except straight ahead after the manner of a horse with blinders.

But childhood has its own way of surmounting difficulties. A few leaps and bounds carried one to the open

The old State House in Concord. *Photo courtesy of the New Hampshire Historical Society.*

air where one could see and breathe once more. The prim bow was soon jerked to nothingness; the long strings gathered into a hard knot at the end left the offending shaker dangling down the back to the limit of its tether.

That first day in school marked an epoch in my life. It was a great step into a new world and yet a natural one. I was fascinated beyond words by what must have been the droning of a primary school of the severe New England type, unrelieved by any of the schoolroom recreations common today, and yet on that first day something caught and held me for life. When the teacher caught me reading the words in the primer, she announced that on the morrow I could enter the First Reader Class.

Between that day and this, there have been other successes, but none stands out more clearly. At dinner (dinner was at noon) I announced after that first half day that when I grew up I was going to be a teacher.

The Parker School. *Photo courtesy of the New Hampshire Historical Society.*

From that early decision there was no wavering until with full vested rights I stood before my first school of some eighty-five little children. This enthusiasm continued for another forty-five years as a teacher.

As I look back, I am convinced that for that time, I might say for any time, this school in Concord was a good one. Here, until I was nine years old, I had only two teachers and they were of the finest type of New England spinsters. I do not remember their names, but I do remember with gratitude the simple, honest direction they gave to my school days. They were as uncompromising as my father in matters of duty and demanded prompt and unquestioning obedience. They were sometimes stricter than modern methods would approve, yet, in retrospect their severity is without condemnation. In two instances only does any feeling of injustice cling to my heart.

The teacher had directed us to sit with folded arms, position one, I think she called it. I fully intended to obey but my curls fell uncomfortably forward about neck and face. It was a stiflingly hot day. I unfolded my arms long enough to brush back the curls and returned immediately to the assigned position, but I had disobeyed a command. For such disobedience, the uniform penalty was to bring the offender out in front of the school and administer six strokes of the ferule on the open palm. I remember counting the strokes, determined not to flinch.

Yes, the penalty was over-severe, but I had disobeyed a definite command and the teacher, without investigation, did not let "mercy season justice." My pride, however, was not seriously wounded for everyone was treated the same, conduct being interpreted strictly according to the letter of the law. Perhaps it was then and there that the lesson of unquestioning obedience to authority was driven home, for somewhere I

95

did learn that lesson early. It may have saved me from serious calamity later. Who knows? The evils we escape unwittingly are never listed.

Another example of this stern discipline clings to memory. One day a little friend and I stayed after school to work out our arithmetic problems for the next day. She, being a thrifty little maiden, copied each example on her own slate as we went along. We were doing the work on my slate so each example was erased as soon as the answer was triumphantly reached. After we had finished, she left and I remained to get my own work ready. First I cleaned my slate with the bottle of colored water that we kept in our desks for that purpose. Mine was blue, I remember. It took me some time to go over the work again and the lateness of the hour made me feel hurried for I was expected home at a very definite hour. In my worry I could not remember one point in the last example. My friend's slate stood on the floor against her desk. I had done most of the work in the first place, so with no thought of cheating, I looked at her slate. The teacher came slowly from the platform, took my slate, and in ruthless silence wiped it clean. She refused to hear my explanation. There could be none for cheating—such was the edict of her New England conscience.

Another picture of school life comes to mind from that dim, uncomplicated era. Valuable and necessary as they are today, there were no laws then promulgated by a Board of Health, and parents were not particularly concerned when their children were afflicted by such "inevitable" diseases as mumps or chickenpox. When I was seven, the school suffered from a rather severe epidemic of mumps. No one thought of staying home if afflicted on one side only and no one had to be told by a doctor what the matter was— mother simply gave the victim a nice spoonful of vinegar and the diagnosis was spontaneous. It *was* considered an act of heroism to have mumps on both sides and not miss a day of school. With pride, I remember accomplishing that feat. I shall never forget the picture of that room during that epidemic. Boys and girls sat with swollen faces tied up in great handkerchiefs of various hues, while frequent groans and grimaces testified to the suffering of the victims.

The standards of this typical New England school were rigid. It was not considered necessary to pay any attention to a child's whims or to entice him into learning through entertaining methods. So far as I can remember, there were no so-called "nervous" children demanding special treatment. If there were they did not get it, and I suppose there may have been casualties that were unknown. We did everything on a precise schedule. At the time set for arithmetic, we did arithmetic. Our moods were not consulted, and we never dreamed that this systematic and definite routine might warp our little souls, nor did our parents worry about the matter.

Arithmetic was very oldfashioned. We learned our multiplication tables by rote, reciting them in a singsong, and said our "fives" faster than the others. We had miles of mental arithmetic, when we had to repeat the example word for word after one reading by the teacher and then go through a prescribed reasoning process to the answer. My aunt assisted this mathematical combat by a game she used to play. She would invite me to take a ride with her. If I could not recite my "tables" to a certain point before we reached our neighbor's house, the horses were turned back and the drive was over that day.

We had a spelling book and learned columns of words with puzzlers like quay, phthisis, and roquelaure where pronunciation gave little clue to the spelling. Our Friday "spell-downs" furnished good training. Standing in a row, toes hugging a chalk mark or crack in the floor, watching with forward bending body those above, with mind alert for a missing vowel or a superfluous consonant that might offer a chance to "go up," made daily and intensive study a necessity. "Leaving off head" was

no great honor, but we worked hard to attain it and our mothers drilled us constantly.

For reading, school boards did not furnish the supplementary readers or the treasure-filled libraries of today. Each child had his own reader and read it over and over again. The stories in it were worth reading, as all McGuffy trained can testify, real stories out of real literature, luring us on to the masterpiece itself, as soon as it could be found. Poetry found ample space in our readers, and many, many of the world's most famous poems became a permanent part of memory and can be recalled at will.

We had much practice in penmanship with insistence that the penholder must point to the right ear. The teacher went about the room turning pens in the right direction, often saying, "What is that pen doing pointing over to Bow Crossing?" I have no idea where "bow crossing" was or is, but I have always meant one day to locate it and see if the teacher's direction was right.

None of the above is put forth as an argument in favor of these old-fashioned methods, for my own teaching wandered far from them, but merely as a record of my own childhood and the school in Concord.

My memory harks back to two especially vivid events of my first year in school. I call these memories,

"My First Crime" and "My First Love Affair." For the first I was never brought to judgment, but no punishment is greater than one's own conscience, especially if one was born and reared in New England.

During my early weeks at school the teacher had made some changes in seats. My new one was on the outside aisle near a window and about three seats from the front. The little girl who had occupied the one assigned to me had removed her reader, her slate with sponge tied to frame, and her bottle of colored water. As I put my own small belongings into the desk, I discovered something wrapped in stiff white paper. I opened it and peeped cautiously. There was a beautiful pink gumdrop with crystals of sugar glittering on its surface while loose crumbs rattled in the paper.

Automatically I popped the sweet morsel into my mouth. I did not set teeth into it, but with New England thrift I allowed it to melt slowly in "linked sweetness drawn out." When nothing was left but a succulent memory, the little girl came back for her pink gumdrop. Had it been there I should have handed it over at once, but it was gone, gone forever, and its sweetness was fast turning to bitterness. A child not yet five years old is not prepared to grapple with ethical questions. I saw no way out but the way of silence, to which I added the cunning of some real crim-inals, by entering into the useless search, for was not the sweet stickiness still on my tongue? The little girl cast one last look into the corners of the desk and went sadly away. To a little girl in the first primary even one gumdrop is a valuable asset. She doubtless forgot the loss very soon, but to this day the sight of a gumdrop recalls the scene and brings back all the misery of that experience. In imagination and in my dreams for many years I bought tons of gumdrops to give the little girl, but I never could remember her name or where in the wide world she disappeared.

The object of my juvenile affections was a little boy a few months older than I. He and the gumdrop girl and my special friend, Ella, are the only children of whom any impression remains from the first school years.

Charlie had beautiful yellow curls that fell to his shoulders in symmetrical ringlets—perhaps an image of Little Lord Fauntleroy. He wore a long-sleeved brown and white checked gingham apron, scanter than a girl's, and fastened with a shiny leather belt. We bestowed various infantile attentions upon each other. At all childrens' parties, he was my Knight and if, by any chance, he seemed to prefer another even for a few minutes, my little heart knew all the torments furnished by the green-eyed monster.

Although I only half understood what the older girls were talking about in whispered excitement as Valentine's Day drew near, I had gathered enough information to know that I must send something to Charlie. Among my treasures was a valentine which until now had meant nothing to me but a pretty bit of color and lacy paper, but on Valentine's Day it sprang to full significance. I longed to send it to Charlie, but I could not write and I had no envelope. Valentine in hand, I followed my mother about the house asking various pertinent questions but I could not find the courage to tell what was on my mind. After amusing herself for a time with my confusion, she got the valentine ready for the mail. I rushed to the Post Office before school. Charlie was there ahead of me, but both of us knew that one should never, never tell, so back to school we flew. Later, however, the secret grew too oppressive to keep and we gradually sidled toward each other and Charlie burst out with "There's something at the Post Office for you," and I replied, "There's something for you too." But we never "told" because neither of us said a word about a valentine.

Soon after this, word raced around school that Charlie was to have a birthday party. His parents lived in a beautiful house. It seemed like a story-book palace compared to our tiny cottage. The fear of not being invited was almost too much to bear. Children whose mothers knew Charlie's mother were sure they would be invited—but my mother did not know her and the girls said that Charlie's people were very, very rich and surely would only invite their own friends. I had never thought about riches before and couldn't see how that could have anything to do with being invited to a party. Charlie and I were best friends and surely friends invited friends to a party, and yet I worried. I was fiercely loyal to my mother, who was so young and so beautiful—much lovelier even than Charlie's mother, in my eyes, so I could not see how mothers could have anything to do with invitations. I had not yet learned that neither beauty nor ability is the key that unlocks the magic door to Society.

However, this story turned out in my favor, for the precious invitation did come and the relief was great. The Saturday came at last. I can remember distinctly the dress I wore. It was white and ruffled with a broad pink sash and shoulder knots of pink fluttering against my neck and arms. There were several starched skirts underneath and my shoes were shiny bright.

His house was a castle that day. The long parlors had been transformed into a garden of beautiful flowers and I walked about in a dream. The party was to begin with a march. Each little boy was instructed to take a partner with Charlie leading. My heart stopped when I heard Charlie's mother call out," Come, Charlie, take Edith and stand in the doorway until we get the others in line." I was trembling—Charlie to take Edith when he and I were Valentines—I wanted to run away, but just then Charlie asserted himself and the velvet suit and yellow curls marched over to me and he announced to his mother, "I am marching with Florence."

I suppose his mother "adjusted" as mothers have had to do both before and after this memorable year of 1861, for, surprised and disap-pointed, perhaps, she was wise, and smiling at us both, said, "Very well. Take Florence and find your place." How proudly we led the march, hand in hand, in and out of the gaily decorated rooms to the dining room where refreshments were served.

There is no sequel to the story. He went his way and I went mine, but the experience, never forgotten, taught me that children are more than children and that not all their thoughts are of dolls, toy trains, and tin soldiers. The emotions may be fleeting, but they are serious and important while they last and call for sympathy and understanding.

CARE OF THE INSANE

Tuesday cloudy morn & fair & pleasant P.M. After breakfast bid adieu to the hospitable family of Dickinsons—had a pleasant ride to Northampton, called at Col Chapmans Tavern. Mr B. went to the Barbers—I went a shopping.— dined with Mrs Pomroy (once Mrs Reed)—at half past two left N Hampton, after viewing externally the Elegant new meeting house—and beautiful seats of the 3 Mr Shepherds and the late Judge Henshaw &c &c—called at Hatfield (a pleasant Town) to see the truly unfortunate Mrs Martin (Once Mr Bascoms Landlady) now in a state of derangement (O piteous sight), chained to the floor—to to [sic] prevent her destroying herself & others! ! ! called at Grimes Tavern in Whately—saw Mrs Levi Bakers niece—then ascended the long hills of Conway &c till at sunset we arrived at the house of Capt Billings, where invited to call & pass the time of our sojourning in this place. . .

MS Journal of Ruth
Henshaw Bascom, 22 June 1813

Connecticut's Black Law

by Frances Edwards

Chaucer's Canterbury Tales are familiar to everyone, at least as a part of literature and history. Connecticut's Canterbury Tale is known to but a few, but as a tale of a heroic conflict of courage, conscience, and calumny it deserves a retelling.

Canterbury is in Windham County, in the eastern part of Connecticut, and it has the features common to many New England towns incorporated in the eighteenth century: a village green, wide street, shade trees, old homes framed in spacious lawns. They give a feeling of security, of things unchanged in a changing world. Canterbury probably does not appear very different today from what it was a hundred and thirty-odd years ago, the time of the Tale.

The automobile has replaced the horse and wagon. Modern conveniences have made the old homes more comfortable, but outwardly the appearance is much the same. The eighteenth-century house built by Squire Elisha Paine, with its beautiful Georgian detail, still overlooks the green and the former Andrew Judson place across the way. Atop the hill the white Congregational Church still points its octagonal spire heavenward.

It was here in the Elisha Paine house that the Tale began in 1831. Before it was finished, two years later, a corrosive black blot had stained Connecticut's history.

Prudence Crandall was twenty-eight years old when she bought the Paine homestead and opened there "A Select School for Females." She was a daughter of Quaker parents and had been reared and educated in the strict discipline of the Society of Friends. The leading families of the town were delighted to have her school in their midst. Andrew Judson, the neighbor across the green, and others of the foremost citizens had encouraged and aided Miss Crandall in this venture.

These men looked with much favor on the quiet, refined young Quakeress. They felt their daughters would benefit greatly from her

Prudence Crandall, oil portrait by Francis Alexander. *Cornell University Library, Samuel May Collection.*

teaching. Also it was a convenient place to send these daughters, a bridge between the district school and marriage. In that day advanced education for young ladies was not deemed necessary. Within a short time the school's capacity was filled, and thus a year passed away.

Not all the young ladies of Canterbury attended the school. Some had no wish to carry on, others were financially unable. There was one among them, however, who sincerely wished to continue her studies. She had been born in the town and had been a classmate of

Miss Crandall's girls in the district school. Her quick, alert mind had merited their admiration on many occasions. Her great ambition was to be sufficiently educated to teach her own race. Her name was Sarah Harris and she was a Negress.

Early in 1832 Sarah called on Miss Crandall and asked permission to enter the school. Knowing the girl's ability and her goal in life, Miss Crandall strongly felt Sarah should have her chance and admitted her to the school.

The first day passed in the usual routine. The other girls accepted Sarah as a matter of course. She was the same girl who had been their classmate in their earlier years.

As was natural, the supper table conversation in many of the Canterbury homes was about the day at Miss Crandall's. This evening the young ladies told their parents about the new pupil admitted that day, Sarah Harris. It was as though a bomb had been dropped. Dessert was forgotten as fathers rushed from their homes to their neighbors. In no time at all a delegation was formed of the so-called leading citizens. The greatest uproar occurred in the Judson household, and it was the Honorable Andrew Judson who led the delegation across the green that very evening to Miss Crandall's. As spokesman for the group, he demanded that she dismiss Sarah Harris.

South view of Canterbury. Arrow at left indicates the school. *Photo courtesy of the Connecticut Historical Society.*

Andrew Judson was not only *the* great man of Canterbury but also one of the state's leading politicians and a Judge of the United States District Court. His word was law, inside and outside the town.

Prudence Crandall, a gentle person by nature and by religious conviction, was not unfamiliar with intolerance, nor with persecution. As she listened to the great Mr. Judson, the fighting spirit inherited from her Quaker folk rose in indignation and she flatly told him that she would not dismiss Sarah. Such defiance was new to the great man; this woman must be taught a lesson, so he delivered his ultimatum — either Sarah Harris would be dismissed or he would use his influence to have all the parents withdraw their daughters.

That night there was great conflict in Prudence's mind. All through the sleepless hours she weighed the pros and cons of the situation. She thought of the expense involved in keeping the school, of the payments which must be met on time. Should she yield to this unfair demand and ensure the financial success of her school? Or should she follow the teachings of her Quaker parents and do what she believed right?

The answer came as the new day was dawning: there could be no compromise. Early that morning Mr. Judson came to hear her decision. She told him, "The school may fail, but I will not fail Sarah Harris." The girl would stay.

Judson took steps at once to carry out his threat. When school opened that morning there was one pupil in attendance, Sarah Harris. One can picture this frail, young schoolmistress, sheltered all her life, defying the powerful leading citizen of that village. She had the courage of her convictions; she was a true follower of Him who said, "Inasmuch as ye have done it unto the least of one of these, my brethren, ye have done it unto Me."

Through the long hours of another wakeful night Prudence thought

103

about her problem. By morning she had come to a momentous decision. She would retain her school; she would keep Sarah Harris, but from now on the only pupils admitted would be "young ladies and little misses of color." This was the wording she used in the advertisement sent to William Lloyd Garrison, the noted Abolitionist, to be inserted in his anti-slavery newspaper, *The Liberator*, published in Boston. Her letter to him, a long one, told the complete story and explained the seemingly strange advertisement.

Within a few days Prudence received Mr. Garrison's reassuring reply. He wrote that full support would be given to her by the leaders of the Abolitionist movement, and the next issue of the *Liberator* would carry her announcement. So it did, with much the same effect on the citizenry of Canterbury as that of a red flag waved before a bull. A storm broke in full fury. A town meeting was hastily called in the staid church atop the hill. From floor to gallery it was packed.

The fathers of the men gathered there had fought together in the Revolution. Many of them had been with old "Put" when he dragged the wolf from the nearby Pomfret den. Now the sons of these men rushed to the meeting from their farms and fields intent on one purpose, to drag the "Quakeress wolf"

PRUDENCE CRANDALL,
Principal of the Canterbury, (Conn.) Female Boarding School,

RETURNS her most sincere thanks to those who have patronized her School, and would give information that on the first Monday of April next, her School will be opened for the reception of young Ladies and little Misses of color. The branches taught are as follows:—Rearding, Writing, Arithmetic, English Grammar, Geography, History, Natural and Moral Philosophy, Chemistry, Astronomy, Drawing and Painting, Music on the Piano, together with the French language.

☞ The terms, including *board, washing,* and tuition, are $25 per quarter, one half paid in advance.

☞ Books and Stationary will be furnished on the most reasonable terms.

For information respecting the School, reference may be made to the following gentlemen, viz:—Arthur Tappan, Esq., Rev. Peter Williams, Rev. Theodore Raymond, Rev. Theodore Wright, Rev. Samuel C. Cornish, Rev. George Bourne, Rev. Mr. Hayborn, *New-York city ;*—Mr. James Forten, Mr. Joseph Cassey, *Philadelphia, Pa. ;*—Rev. S. J. May, *Brooklyn, Ct. ;*—Rev. Mr. Beman, *Middletown, Ct. ;*—Rev. S. S. Jocelyn, *New-Haven, Ct. ;*—Wm. Lloyd Garrison, Arnold Buffum, *Boston, Mass. ;*—George Benson, *Providence, R. I.*   Canterbury, (Ct.) Feb. 25, 1833.

First appearance of Prudence Crandall's advertisement in the *Liberator*, Mar. 2, 1833.

from her den. The meeting was hectic. Resolutions were quickly made and as quickly passed. In long speeches Prudence Crandall was denounced violently and abusively.

Prudence calmly continued her plans for the new venture. There had been offers of help from Boston and New York Abolitionists, as Garrison had assured her there would be. The Reverend Samuel J. May of the nearby town of Brooklyn was at hand, with spiritual encouragement, while Arthur Tappan, a wealthy New York merchant, stood ready with financial aid. The battle was on.

On the appointed day, as stated in the *Liberator's* announcement, Miss Crandall's school reopened. There were twenty pupils in attendance, all "little misses of color."

The great Mr. Judson was furious. Again he had been openly defied by a lone, gentle woman. But, he was by no means done with the matter. On his order another town meeting was called, more resolutions made and passed, and more speeches delivered, much more drastic, in their gross misrepresentations, concerning Miss Crandall. Judson in his speech made no attempt to conceal the hostility he felt for his neighbor across the green and openly declared his intentions to thwart her plans.

On behalf of Prudence, the Reverend Mr. May attended this meeting and made a vain attempt to speak in her defense. He was quickly shouted down and held there by law, which gave the right to speak to town citizens only. There was nothing now to be done but wait.

In a few days, the path the town would take was clearly visible. There was no signpost to mark it, but that boycott was its name was apparent. The merchants of Canterbury refused to sell anything at all to Prudence or to anyone connected with her school. She was not able to buy food or other supplies of any kind. One night one of her "little misses of color" was taken suddenly ill; she called in the local doctor, who refused to attend the child or to come to the school. Judson's power was great enough to make a medical man forget his Hippocratic oath.

Prudence a few days later was made to realize fully how completely the power and influence of the great Judson had blanketed the town of Canterbury. On Sunday when she and her pupils came to attend the service at the church on the hill, the doors were locked and they were refused admittance.

During this time of stress and strain, Prudence's brother, Hezekiah, and her father brought food and other supplies to the school weekly. As soon as the Judson followers found out they tried by threats and fines to scare them away. The threats had no effect and the fines were paid without argument through funds furnished by Mr. Tappan and others. The cold war had now developed into a twenty-four-hour siege.

The students needed exercise, and it was Miss Crandall's custom to take them to walk each day. There was no place to go except through the town, and it can be truthfully said that each day they walked a gauntlet. Their ears heard the verbal insults from all sides, and their bodies felt the mud balls and other missiles thrown at them by the town's youth. The press carried fantastic and untrue stories about the whole unfortunate affair, and no newspaper dared refute them.

Judson probably remained awake at night thinking of ways and means to win this battle. He would not be content until he had driven Prudence and her school from the town. His position as leading citizen would be in jeopardy until this was accomplished, to say nothing of the slight to his ego. He looked over some of the old colonial laws, still on the statute books though not enforced for many years. One seemed to fit the situation, so Prudence was duly "warned out of town." This law had been useful in the colonial period to keep undesirable transients from settling in a town, particularly if they were apt to become public charges. The penalty for not heeding the warning was public whipping.

Prudence did not heed it, and in order to save face Judson had to make some pretense of carrying out the penalty. One of the school's pupils offered to take the whipping, and again Judson was forced to retreat with as much grace as he could muster. He now realized that the whole affair could boomerang.

Meanwhile the young people of the town, aided and abetted by their elders, were making the most of any opportunity to harass the occupants of the Paine house. Time and again they spattered the framework with rotten eggs. Under cover of darkness they sent a barrage of stones sailing through the windows and on another occasion they filled the well with dung. The well was the only source of water, but just as the window glass was patiently replaced many times, so the father and brother of Prudence added water to their weekly load.

The school was continuing daily in a fairly normal way. By her teaching and example Prudence kept the children's spirit toward their persecutors free from bitterness and hate. Each day, as a closing exercise, they sang the hymn she taught them.

But, we forgive
Forgive the men who persecute us so
May God, in mercy, save their souls
From everlasting woe.

As time went on and Judson saw no victory in sight, it became evident that new and different measures must be used. Through his influence, the General Assembly of Connecticut passed a law, May 24, 1833, which "forbid any person, under severe penalty, from establishing, in any town in Connecticut, without the written permit of the Selectmen, a school, for the education of colored people, and from teaching, boarding or harboring the same." History records this law as the Black Law, that is a law concerning Negroes, but the law also blackened the name of the state.

The clause in the law "under severe penalty" would have intimidated most people, but not the quiet, gentle, Quaker girl. She continued her daily tasks, her daily walks, her daily routine unmoved, outwardly at least. When it became clear to the townspeople that she did not intend to close her school or to leave the place, she was arrested and brought to trial.

Again Mr. Tappan came forward with aid. He hired for her defense three of the ablest lawyers in the state, Calvin Goodard, William W. Ellsworth, and Henry Strong. They proved themselves worthy. Their arguments were so logical and forceful that the jury could not agree, though sent back three times.

Again Prudence was brought to trial, this time convicted by the State Supreme Court, which sentenced her to jail. The Judson forces felt certain her Abolitionist friends would come forward with bail money so that the ignominy of sending a woman to jail on such a charge would not rest on them. And so those friends would have furnished bail, gladly, but Prudence refused to accept it. She knew that being in jail would help her cause far more. Her lawyers then entered an appeal. Prudence stayed in jail just long enough to worry her persecutors, and was then released on bail. Her case was now brought to the Court of Errors, highest legal tribunal in the state.

The jail sentence, combined with the other aspects of the case, had brought public opinion to the front. The whole matter was fast getting out of hand, and to such an extent that rather than be committed to a decision, a technical informality was found in the indictment; that ended the court business.

During the days of her trial, Prudence had noticed a tall, distinguished-looking gentleman among the spectators. Although he was a complete stranger to her, his sympathetic look gave her the feeling he was a friend. During a court recess he was introduced to her by one of her lawyers as the Reverend Calvin Philleo, a Baptist minister of Suffield. He had been drawn to the trial by the strong sympathy he felt for her and her cause. Their acquaintance ripened quickly, admiration turned to love, and within a short time Prudence Crandall became Mrs. Philleo.

Married to this strong, devout man, Prudence felt encouraged to carry on her chosen work. Now that the court case was dismissed and there seemed to be no further methods of persecution, she looked forward to peaceful days.

Her nature was not vindictive; she could forgive those who had wronged her and try to forget. It was soon clear, however, that the quiet was the calm before the storm.

One night the household awakened to the smell of smoke. It took all their combined efforts to extinguish a fire which had had a good start in one section of the old home. The evidence clearly pointed to arson. Prudence and her little household knew it could happen again, a knowledge that was not conducive to restful sleep. Next time they might not be so lucky.

After another short interval of quiet, again their sleep was shattered, this time by a terrific noise. The frightened group were soon aware that an attack was being made on the old Paine homestead, simultaneously from all sides. The men and boys of the town armed with heavy clubs and iron bars were breaking doors, windows and any other part of the old house that would yield to their strength. Then, when the destruction had been completed to their satisfaction, they slipped away in the darkness. The shaken and dazed group within, down to the smallest "little miss of color," realized this was the end.

The attack was the final straw in seventeen months of continuous persecution by town and state. Prudence Crandall Philleo, gazing around at the destruction of her home, knew she had reached the limit of human endurance. She

Congregationalist Meetinghouse, Canterbury.

began the preparations to close the school and the house and withdraw.

These long months of struggle had been watched from far and near. Now, too late to help the courageous Quaker girl, the finger of shame was raised in the direction of Canterbury from every point of the compass. Judson had won the victory, if it could be called that, but its sweetness was removed by the scorn. Before the accusations and the scorn were forgotten another generation was to grow to maturity in Canterbury. Judson would be asleep in the churchyard, atop the hill, without having sat in the coveted governor's chair, which at one time had seemed so close.

It took twenty-eight years and the

Civil War to lower this finger of shame. It is said that truth is stranger than fiction. This old adage was proved in the war years, when Windham became the banner county of the state. A year after the war ended, in 1866, Windham County voted not only for Negro education, but for complete Negro suffrage as well.

* * * *

News of the county's action came to Prudence Crandall Philleo in far-off Illinois. There she had been teaching and her minister husband preaching for many years, following a work and a way of life pleasing to both. More happiness was hers when a leading speaker of the day declared:

> This Quaker girl, shut out of one town, for teaching 20 colored children, arithmetic, grammar and astronomy, taught all the people of the County's 15 towns, and helped in teaching the whole state, one of the grandest lessons, in Liberty Civilization, and Morals, that America has ever had. She taught the arithmetic, which counts souls; the grammar, which speaks correctly, the language of Freedom; and the Astronomy, which deals with the eternal stars of love and duty.

Calvin Philleo died in 1874.

Prudence then removed to Elk Falls, Kansas, to spend her remaining years with her brother, the same Hezekiah who had helped keep the school supplied with the necessaries of life so long ago.

Final honor came to her in 1886, just three years before her death. The General Assembly of Connecticut was again petitioned in her case, again by the people of Canterbury. The sons of the men who had petitioned to have her banished from the town now petitioned to grant her a pension. Many of these petitioners of 1886 had undoubtedly been among the youths who had done so much damage in the earlier years. Now, actuated by mature thought and tolerance, they were seeking to right an old wrong:

> We, the undersigned, citizens of this state, and of the town of Canterbury, mindful of the dark blot, that rests upon our fair name and fame, for the cruel outrages inflicted upon a former citizen of our commonwealth, a noble, Christian woman . . . .

The petition was granted and a pension given to Prudence. At last she knew how great was the admiration held for her by the people of Connecticut.

The First Oekologist

by Francis E. Wylie

For a married woman to achieve not only bliss but intellectual parity with her husband a hundred years ago was a remarkable accomplishment. Ellen Swallow's love affair with Robert H. Richards was hardly one of history's great romances, but it demonstrated that hearts and minds could be equal, rational, and compatible.

Ellen Swallow, a liberated female for her day, was the first woman student at the Massachusetts Institute of Technology and she became a fine chemist, a crusader for good food, clean air, and pure water, and the mother of "domestic science."

Robert Richards, a member of the first class at M.I.T., was a pioneer in modern metallurgy and had the perspicacity to admit science to the domestic scene. He and Nellie, as he called her, made a remarkable team.

Ellen was born in Dunstable, Massachusetts, in the hills near the New Hampshire border. Her father was a farmer-storekeeper-teacher, and after she had attended Westford Academy she herself taught for a while. By the time she was twenty-six she was sickly in health and clearly destined to be an old maid. Then, apparently in a sudden burst of determination, she pulled herself together and, with her scanty savings and borrowed money, financed her admission to Vassar College in 1868.

Vassar, which had opened only three years before, the first women's college of consequence, revealed a new world to Miss Swallow. "Some twenty or more of the girls wear their hair flowing to their waists without any attempt at doing it up," she wrote in her diary, a bit priggishly, at the end of her first week. "It is not usually curly, but long and straight. It seems as if they had not yet dressed."

Being older than other Vassar girls, and more serious, she had no time for fashion and frivolity. She worked her way to a degree by tutoring, and then decided she wanted to be a chemist. She was advised that the best and perhaps only place to study chemistry was the Massachusetts Institute of Technology, already recognized as a first-rate scientific school though it had opened the same year as Vassar, 1865.

Ellen Swallow as a college student.

M.I.T. was a college for men. Women were admitted to a night class in chemistry taught by Charles W. Eliot (who left the faculty in 1869 to become president of Harvard), but those who had applied for status as full-time students were rebuffed. Miss Swallow had special qualifications, however, and the Institute agreed in 1871 to take her as a special student — without fees, so she would not officially be enrolled. That suited Ellen, and within a month she wrote:

I am winning a way which others will keep open. Perhaps the fact that I am not a Radical or a believer in the all powerful ballot for women to right her wrongs and that I do not scorn womanly duties, but claim it as a privilege to clean up and sort of supervise the room and sew things, etc., is winning me stronger allies than anything else. Even Prof. A. accords me his sanction when I sew his papers or tie up a sore finger or dust the table, etc. Last night Prof. B. found me useful to mend *his suspenders* which had come to grief.

Prof. B. presumably was Bob Richards, in whose laboratory Ellen was shut up "very much as a dangerous animal" to keep her from contact with undergraduate men. He was three years younger than she and a first-year faculty member.

Richards had been born in Gardiner, Maine. His mother's family background included the wealthy Gardiners, Tudors, and Hallowells, and his father was the son of an English merchant. He had gone to school in England, was invariably defeated by Greek and Latin, failed to get into Harvard, and was at the foot of his class at Phillips Exeter Academy when he heard about M.I.T. — a new kind of college. He was one of the first seven students to enter.

M.I.T. was innovating — teaching science in the laboratory. "The method of teaching was completely new to all of us," Richards later recalled. "We found ourselves bidding goodby to the old learn-by-heart method, and begging to study by observing the facts and laws of nature."

I found that this new school was teaching me nature, which I had loved and observed all my life; that I was being taught nature by direct contact

The first M.I.T. building on Boylston Street, Boston, from the 1870-71 catalogue.

and that mathematics, languages and history, were nothing but a means to an end. Having at last found out the use of books, I could not read or study enough to satisfy my craving for knowledge, experience and skill. In academic schools, I had to drag myself to my books, never understanding why I must. Now I could not keep away from books, drawing board and laboratory. Education ceased to be a plague spot and became a delight."

Richards graduated in 1868 with a degree in geology and mining engineering and immediately became an instructor. In 1871 he organized what was probably the first laboratory in the world in which ore could be processed by industrial methods. His classmate, Joseph Revere (grandson of Paul), came in from the Revere Copper Company plant at Canton, Massachusetts, to show him how to smelt copper.

That same year Richards participated in what was probably the first summer school of its kind. He and his M.I.T. students traveled on the new transcontinental railroad to mines and smelters in the western mountains in order to study methods and they brought back more than 200 bags of ore to work with in the laboratory. For thirty years Richards conducted such expeditions in all parts of the country.

To maintain the fiction that she was not a student, Ellen Swallow had been listed at M.I.T. as "not a candidate for a degree" but in 1873 she was awarded the degree of Bachelor of Science (and also an A.M. by Vassar). In the laboratory a few days later, Professor Richards asked her to become his wife.

"To my everlasting joy, she decided to accept my offer," Professor Richards wrote. They were married two years later and Nellie donned boots and a short skirt to spend the honeymoon with mining students on a trip to Nova Scotia. By buckboard and muleback, Mrs. Richards and her husband visited lead, copper, tin, silver, gold, and iron mines during succeeding summers. She was chemist for the team and she was the first woman to be elected to the American Institute of Mining Engineers. She was also elected a fellow of the American Association for the Advancement of Science, an unusual honor for that time.

This was a period of enormous development in mining, and Professor Richards was a consultant to such companies as the fabulous Calumet and Hecla in finding new deposits and solving processing problems. He invented machinery and wrote the definitive four-volume, 2,800-page work on ore-dressing.

New England mineral inspectors had occasionally induced gold fever in the inhabitants; Professor Richards showed their optimism to be unjustified. Discovery of gold and silver near Newburyport set people frantically to digging up pastures and resulted in the sale of a million dollars in stock. Richards demonstrated that only a shallow vein existed — not enough to pay for the mining.

At another time, Richards was persuaded to examine ore displayed by some promoters who exhibited receipts from the New York Mint indicating that they had shipped $80,000 in pure gold. Richards was suspicious and found (with a taste test) that the ore consisted of rocks covered with flour paste into which some gold dust had been introduced. With money from the sale of stock, the promoters had melted up gold coins to provide the dust as well as some genuine gold bricks to be shipped to the Mint. Pure fraud.

After her graduation from M.I.T., Ellen Swallow was appointed an assistant in chemistry and later, instructor. She wanted to get a doctorate, a degree not yet awarded by the Institute, but came up against an insurmountable academic wall. Years later, Professor Richards reflected that the faculty shrank from the prospect of letting a woman be the first doctor of science produced by M.I.T.

It was 1883 before women were admitted to M.I.T. on equal footing with men. Mrs. Richards served unofficially as their dean, while supervising a Woman's Laboratory which was especially effective in training teachers of chemistry.

Much of her time, however, went into the study of pollution and public health hazards. Typhoid fever and other diseases were constant menaces, and the Massachusetts Board of Health commissioned an M.I.T. professor to survey sources of drinking water, many of them contaminated by sewage. Mrs. Richards did most of the laboratory work and through three decades performed thousands of analyses of water from all parts of the state. When the world's first comprehen-

Ellen Swallow Richards (extreme left rear) with women students of M.I.T., 1888.

sive course in sanitary engineering was inaugurated, she was one of the key teachers. She also studied air pollution, examined wallpapers and textiles for arsenic, and analyzed foods for adulterants.

Years earlier when she had been a student at Vassar, Ellen had been convinced of the importance of fresh air by a professor's demonstration that lighted candles placed in a closed container would be extinguished for lack of oxygen. She wrote (with the prevalent lack of understanding of the nature of tuberculosis): "Consumption is the result of the tight building of the present day. A fireplace is better than life insurance."

People at that time were walling up fireplaces and installing stoves. They kept their windows closed while they slept for fear of "night air." Mrs. Richards crusaded for good ventilation in homes and schools. She and her husband installed special ventilators in their own home in Boston. In fact, their

house became a kind of laboratory for testing new ideas in cookery and homemaking.

Mrs. Richards favored education for women on general principles but she directed her energies toward improving their education in the practical application of science to home management. The creative arts, such as spinning and weaving, had been taken out of the home, leaving women with the dull drudgery of cleaning and cooking without an understanding of how domestic life could be improved. In a talk before the women of Poughkeepsie in 1879, the first of many addresses she would make throughout the country, Mrs. Richards said:

Now it is often stated that our educational system unfits the girls for their work in life, which is largely that of housekeepers. It cannot be the knowledge that unfits them. One can never know too much of things which one is to handle. . . . Can a cook know too much about the composition and nutritive

Robert H. Richards (front center) with a group of mining students in 1888.

value of the meats and vegetables which she uses? Can a housekeeper know too much of the effect of fresh air on the human system, of the danger of sewer gas, of foul water?

Go where you will into the country and you will find the sewing machine universal, but alas! just as much poor bread, just as much fried pork, just the same open sink drain under the kitchen window, just the same damp, dark cellar, just as much fear of fresh air, as you would have found thirty years ago. And in the cities, how much better is it; rather, how much worse?

With an understanding of chemistry, Mrs. Richards pointed out, women could detect and battle against adulterants in foods. She herself led a task force in collecting samples from groceries throughout Massachusetts and found, for example, baking powder that was forty-five percent starch and cinnamon that was mostly mahogany sawdust.

To demonstrate to the undernourished poor the value of inexpensive but well-prepared foods, Mrs. Richards opened in Boston a New England Kitchen which sold such dishes as fish chowder at twelve cents and mush at five cents a quart. Similar kitchens were established in Providence, in New York, and at Hull House in Chicago. Mrs. Richards argued that a dime's worth of beans was as nutritious as twenty-five to fifty cents' worth of potatoes (the Irish immigrants' staple). Affluent but frugal Bostonians were good customers, but the people for whom the kitchens were intended were less responsive; the facilities were given up as failures.

"Their death knell was sounded," Mrs. Richards explained, "by the woman who said, 'I don't want to eat what's good for me; I'd ruther eat what I'd ruther.' "

Ellen Richards taking a water sample from a pond.

As a part of the Massachusetts exhibit at the Chicago World's Fair in 1893, Mrs. Richards operated a "Rumford Kitchen," named for the Yankee-born Count Rumford who had pioneered in the science of nutrition. Visitors could watch the expert preparation of food and buy 979.3 calories' worth of baked beans, brown bread, butter, and applesauce for thirty cents.

The year before, Mrs. Richards had coined the word "oekology" (she later spelled it "ecology," but it would not become a household word for more than a half century). She used it to denote the science of housekeeping — ranging from dietetics to sanitary plumbing. "Oekology is the worthiest of all the applied sciences, the science which teaches the principles on which to found healthy and happy homes," she declared. The new word represented Ellen Richards' continuing effort to broaden the scope and rationalize the methods of household technology. The term "domestic science" had been in use for some years — and no one did more to apply science to domestic practices than Mrs. Richards. She organized the domestic science course at the new Pratt Institute in New York and was influential in shaping such studies in other schools and colleges.

In high schools, domestic science had developed somewhat in parallel with manual training for boys; its approach was inadequate, Mrs. Richards thought. Looking backward in 1908, she said:

Ten years ago domestic science meant to most people lessons in cooking and sewing given to classes of the poorer children supported by charitable people, in order to enable them to teach their parents to make a few pennies go as far as a dollar spent in the shops. To

116

do this, common American foods were cooked in American ways, regardless of the nationality of the children, and usually failed to please the inherited foreign tastes. But complacent philanthropists felt happy in having offered bread to the starving, as they were pictured to be, and pretty bad bread it often was, judged by European standards....

So also the tradition of the valuelessness of a woman's time kept the plain sewing to the front, and classes were taught seams and ruffles and cheap ornamentation in the false assumption that it was economy. As late as the St. Louis Exposition, in 1903, the work of the public schools of this country was almost without exception bad from an ethical point of view, showing waste of time and material and the inculcation of bad taste.

It was with this view of the field that Mrs. Richards accepted an invitation in 1898 to visit Melvil Dewey at Lake Placid. Dewey, then director of the state library and of home education in New York (and inventor of the Dewey Decimal library system), needed her advice regarding "Household Science" questions to be incorporated in the New York State regents' college entrance examinations. Out of their conversations grew the concept of "Home Economics," the broader approach that Mrs. Richards had been seeking. A specific result was an invitation to the teachers and writers in the field to a Lake Placid Conference on Home Economics

the next year. The conference, held annually, grew in size and influence under the leadership of Mrs. Richards until, meeting at Chautauqua in 1908, the participants agreed to gather again in Washington later that year to form the American Home Economics Association. Mrs. Richards was elected president and served until 1910, when she insisted on retiring.

The AHEA brought together people with many interests, such as dairying, hygiene, sociology, and economics, and promoted teaching in the field in colleges and schools; sponsored research in nutrition by the United States Department of Agriculture and other agencies; encouraged new kinds of activities by the Grange and women's clubs. It was concerned not only with household science but with the full range of economics of production and consumption.

Mrs. Richards' vision continued to expand. Her first book, published in 1882, *The Chemistry of Cooking and Cleaning: A Manual for Housekeepers*, had been narrowly pragmatic. Through the years she dealt in a practical way with diet, shelter, food adulteration, sanitation, water, and such subjects. Her eighteenth and last book, published in 1911, was titled *Conservation by Sanitation*. But a volume published the previous year showed the extent of her growth. It was titled *Euthenics — The Science of Controlla-*

The Richards at their home, c. 1904.

ble Environment, A Plea for Better Living Conditions as a First Step Toward Higher Human Development.

Mrs. Richards conceived of Euthenics as a way of trying to improve the total environment, of dealing with disease, pollution, crime, moral decay, and all the other physical and spiritual ills of civilization:

America today is wasting its human possibilities even more prodigiously than its material wealth. In the confusion of ideas resulting from the rapid, almost cancerous growth . . . made possible by mechanized invention, the people have lost sight of their own conception of right and wrong.

Here in America we are always locking the barn door after the horse has been stolen. . . . Time presses! A whole generation has been lost because the machine ran wild without guidance.

She believed that government and industry would have to assume responsibilities for improvements, but her hope of salvation lay in education rather than legislation. "Evolution from within, not a dragging from the outside, even if it is in the right direction, is the right method of human development," she asserted.

Like Oekology, Euthenics did not really catch on, although, as the decades passed, mounting social and environmental crises intensified efforts to find solutions. For a number of years Vassar College conducted a Summer Institute for Euthenics. Today there is an International Institute of Euthenics, with headquarters in Chicago. And the word is in the dictionary.

Although she had become a national figure through her crusading, Mrs. Richards continued to devote much of her time to teaching and research at M.I.T. and to helping with local problems. She was the leader in a movement to improve conditions in Boston schools where fire hazards, bad sanitation, poor ventilation, and ill-prepared lunches endangered the lives of children. She was active in other causes, one of them the efforts of the Massachusetts Cremation Society to popularize the new rational method of dealing with dead bodies. Professor Robert Richards visited crematories in other cities to study the various systems, and in Boston an oil-fired method was developed. A large pig was cremated to show that the method was effective, and Professor Richards kept some of its ashes in a toy pig on the mantel of their home.

Mrs. Richards died in 1911, at the age of sixty-eight, following a heart attack. Her ashes were buried at Gardiner, Maine, where her husband had inscribed on a stone:

Pioneer — Educator — Scientist — An Earnest Seeker — A Tireless Worker — A Thoughtful Friend — A Helper of Mankind.

Professor Richards lived on past his hundredth birthday. When he died in 1945 his ashes were also buried at Gardiner.

"I never spend an afternoon with Miss Louisa _____, without being both instructed and delighted. I never take a walk with her in the garden, but she unfolds a thousand, natural curiosities, which had hitherto escaped my unscienced or inattentive eyes. I never ramble with her into the fields, but she gives me such an history of the most common plants and flowers, as at once surprises my curiosity, and gratifies my taste. In her closet she has a large collection of insects, which her microscope clothes with most exquisite beauty, and a museum, filled with shells, corals, and petrifactions, the sparkling of which is exceeded by nothing, but the vivacity of her eyes, or the stronger or more permanent lustre of her virtues.

I would infinitely rather have her taste, than her fortune. And I never quit her without secretly envying her enjoyments. She is ever sprightly because she has never a moment *unemployed*. She always smiles, because she is always innocent. Her pleasures are of the rational and refined kind. They never leave a thorn in the heart or pluck one, blushing rose from her cheeks. How solid and how calm, if compared with the midnight revels of fashion, or the giddiness of admiration!"

John Bennett, *Letters to a Young Lady* (Brattleboro, Vt., 184-), pp. 93-94.

Joseph Palmer and His Famous Beard

by Alfred F. Rosa

In the front row of Evergreen Cemetery in North Leominster, Massachusetts, stands a monument marking the final resting place of Joseph Palmer (1789–1869), protagonist in one of the most unusual episodes in early-nineteenth-century American history. On the front of the stone, beneath a likeness of Palmer with his full beard, reads the inscription "Persecuted for Wearing the Beard." No satisfactory study has ever related the growth of beards or the shaving habits of American men to the political or social climate in which they lived, but if such a study were ever attempted Joseph Palmer would surely have to be given consideration.

Palmer's ancestors came to this country in 1730. His father fought in the Revolutionary War and Palmer himself was a soldier in the War of 1812. He lived in NoTown, so named because it was a gore, a tract of unreclaimed land near Leominster and Fitchburg granted by the General Court to Captain Noah Wiswell for his valor in fighting the Indians. As a descendant of Captain Wiswell, Joseph Palmer inherited the property. It was because he was from NoTown that he first attracted attention to himself, and it may be argued that his whole personality was affected in some incalculable way by his being from "nowhere" as it were. There were those who claimed that his marriage to Nancy Tenney would not be legal because without a meetinghouse in NoTown no marriage banns could be published. Undaunted, Palmer tacked the banns to a huge pine tree near his house and the court agreed that, however peculiar such a procedure, it did accomplish its aim in the eyes of the law.

Palmer's real troubles began when he returned, unshaven, from a hunting trip and continued to grow his beard. During this period it was generally considered that no one except Jews wore beards; the sobriquet "Old Jew Palmer" consequently was given him. Indeed, beards were so rare that "in 1794 a Philadelphia woman wrote that she had seen an elephant and two bearded men on the same remarkable day." It was not until after his inauguration that President Lincoln began to sport a beard, and no likeness of Uncle Sam before 1858 shows him bearded. Despite the hirsute faces of Civil War generals and soldiers and of American authors after mid century, it was considered sinful if not thoroughly satanic to wear a beard in 1830. Acceptance of Palmer and his beard was not aided by society's reaction to the only other local beard on record at the time, that of Silas Lampson, a scythe-snath maker who lived in Sterling. "Old Jew Lampson" was regarded as a fool and thought to be crazy. His own son was afraid to venture anywhere with him for fear of being attacked. Lampson, a religious monomaniac was fond of dressing in white and using "aye" and "nay."

Palmer was jeered and sneered at because of his beard. People hooted at him, brought their unruly children into line with threats that "Old Jew Palmer" would get them, and listened with delight as area clergymen railed against him for his sinful ways. Much of the history of these events comes to us through an 1884 *Boston Daily Globe* interview with Palmer's son Thomas, a Fitchburg dentist, who, like Lampson's son, was guilty by reason of birth and rejected along with his father. Thomas, pleased that history had vindicated his father, told of a confrontation between his father and the Reverend George Trask. The minister asked, "Palmer, why don't you shave and not go round looking like the devil?" Trask was not joking or using a figure of speech in his question, as is indicated by the seriousness of Palmer's answer and the persecutions he would later suffer. He replied, "Mr. Trask, are you not mistaken in your comparison of personages? I have never seen a picture of the ruler of the sulphurous regions with much of a beard, but if I remember correctly, Jesus wore a beard not unlike mine." Such common sense based on scriptural authority was difficult to refute and there was no answer from Trask. Obviously the beard was not evil in itself, but Trask must have thought it symbolized a certain degree of rebelliousness, although there is no historical evidence to show Palmer as anything but an upright citizen. He could cite numerous scriptural passages in support of his refusal to shave, was extremely devout, and attended church regularly, facts which must have disturbed Trask more than a little. Despite such devoutness, Palmer was deeply hurt when he attended a church in Fitchburg where Communion was being offered and he was ignored. When the minister passed over him, Palmer became so indignant that he marched up to the Sacrament table, partook of the offerings, and, turning to the shocked clergyman and his congregation, pronounced, "I love my Jesus as well, and better, than any of you do."

Thomas tells of the event that led to his father's imprisonment:

One day, as father was coming out of the old Fitchburg Hotel, where he had been to carry some provision, he then being in the butchering business, he was seized by four men, whose names I have not in mind now, who were armed with shears, lather, and razor, their intention being to shave him.... These four men laid violent hands on him and threw him heavily on the stone steps, badly hurting his back. The assaulted party was very muscular, and struggled to free himself, but to no purpose, until he drew from his vest pocket an old, loose-jointed jack-knife, with which he struck out left and right and stabbed two of them in the legs, when the assailants precipitately departed without cutting a hair.

As a result of this incident, which took place on May 3, 1830, Palmer was arrested and charged with unprovoked assault and was temporarily jailed at the Fitchburg Hotel-Town Jail. There he began a sequence of demands and disobedient acts that would finally cause his jailers more aggravation than satisfaction.

Suffering from the injury to his back sustained in the scuffle and from a bladder disorder that had bothered him most of his life, Palmer demanded aid and comfort from his jailers. He copied into his daybook (1820–1833) the substance of a letter he wrote to Justice David Brigham stating that he was "in a suffering condition and in [his] sentence" and that he was in need of help. Although not having been formally sentenced and therefore technically free, he was shown little sympathy. Sometime late in May he was taken to the Worcester Jail where he waited almost a month before he was tried. He chose not to pay the ten-dollar fine imposed on him and continued to be the unpopular guest he had been all that preceding month. He refused to eat the prison food, constantly called Bellows, a local tavern keeper who served as county jailer, and the High Sheriff to see him, and demanded that a doctor visit him regularly.

Palmer kept an accurate and detailed diary while in prison. It was written in pencil in a minute, scribbly hand, and its obscurities may have been the result of his keeping the diary surreptitiously. Knowing his keepers as we do from the diary, it is unlikely that they would have let him keep it if they had known of it. Palmer portrays himself in his daily accounts as benignly forceful, stalwart, and of good spirits generally, despite the inhumane treatment he received while in the jail. He was naturally the object of all kinds of curiosity seekers who peered at him through his cell door. He frequently had no control over his bladder and was belittled for wetting the floor of his cell, was on one occasion spat upon, and was generally "black-guarded," as he put it. Palmer's diaries are erratically written in matters of spelling and punctuation. In quoting from his writing, I have sought to maintain his personality as revealed there and to make only those editorial changes necessary for greater clarity. Here follows Palmer's entry for Wednesday, September 22, 1830:

Between 6 and 9 o'clock I heard some person which I thought to be Wilder [jail tender] come into the upper rooms with water and went quick out and soon come in again. I then called Wilder 3 or 4 times but had no answer. I then called Bellows [Asahel Bellows, the jailer] too. Wilder immediately opened the door into the entry next to my door and said What do you want? I said I want you to send me some person to the door here that will go to Mr. Willson's for me and I will pay them just what they ask to copy a few lines. I was just going to ask him for a little water to use until I could get some tea from Willsons as he let a pailfull come in at the demand at full force. It didn't wet me much as I see it was coming and having seen them throw cider and water in the prisoners' faces before it caused me to start so quick there did but little go into my face or on my close, but it went more than half the length of the room. I split three crackers and put them a soak where there was a considerable water stood on the floor, as I could see no chance of getting any other soon. I got a quart jug filled with water out of the other room to wet some bread which was all the water or drink of any kind that I had to use since last Thursday morning when I used the last of my tea, and I had tried ever since Sunday morning to get some and could not. I thought I must suffer very much soon if there wasn't some attention, and

being dissatisfied that there were some in prison who were suffering greatly I thought it time to give a signal of distress to the Publick which I immediately did by the cry of Murder in the Jail.

On July 21, 1830 he records the talk of another attempt to shave him and the winning of an ally:

C.B. began damning me and blackguarding me about my beard. He said if you (I suppose he meant Dike [a fellow prisoner]) will take it off, I will stand and look on all the time and I [will] sware you never touched it. Dike said that's right. I love to here you talk so. By God I wish it was off, and I believe if I was out I could get money enough given me in this street to pay all the damage I should have to pay for doing it. Wilder had come with cider. He said God I guess you could, pretty quick too. Dike said he'd be damned if we don't have it off some how or other. I told C.B. I knew they would swear so here, and now you begin to own it. Wilder said, can't you shear it off when he is a sleep. I told Wilder of an imediate power which he said he knew or could prevent. Dike said damn him he is always awake. F.A. brought the diners of fresh meat, soup, bread, and potatoes, for the other four. C.B. ordered me to hand out the dish I had kept for my porage. I told him I wished he would let me have one that I could keep after I had got it clean. Dike continued in great rage and spite towards me, damning and swearing at me until they come and let us into our room again, when he found out they had got his raisor and sisters. It turned his spite all towards them and before bedtime he was as good towards me as ever a man ought to be to another and talked verry freely with me on the

Power and the Goodness of God and on the Holy Scriptures.

Shortly after his incarceration at the Worcester County Jail, Palmer's wife and son rented rooms near the institution. Being unable to eat the prison food, Palmer requested that his son and wife bring him provisions. For a little over three months, from September 22 to December 25, 1830, the prisoner was kept in solitary confinement. The confinement was not absolute; Palmer had visitors but was separated from the other prisoners. The reasons for this are unclear. There may have been either some threat to his life or fear that he would encourage further disobedience in the jail.

Palmer stayed longer than he was required to by law. He had to pay for his own keep and did not think that such payment was just. Margaret Palmer, his mother, pleaded with him "Not to be so set" and to petition for his release, which he finally did on August 27, 1831. He was granted his freedom shortly thereafter, as he notes that he spent all of September 1 at home. There is some confusion concerning the circumstances of Palmer's release, however. His son Thomas reports that he was such an annoyance to the sheriff and jailers that he was forcefully evicted, the jailers having to carry him from the jail in a chair. While such an incident may have occurred it does seem odd that Palmer did not record it in his diary. Palmer suffered

greatly at the hands of his jailers. He had provoked them continually, making his stay all the more unpleasant. He was a man of principle, however. It was very much in character that he should return to the place that had given him so much pain in order to help the other prisoners. Unfortunately, records regarding the length of his stay at Worcester Jail and the success of his attempts to help the prisoners are unavailable.

Joseph Palmer was not heard from again until the founding of Bronson Alcott's Fruitlands at Harvard, Massachusetts. This utopian community, which sought to create a New Eden and return its members, or consociates, to a state of innocence, needed Palmer's very practical counsel and his expertise and muscle as a farmer. When farming equipment was needed, Palmer would take a trip to NoTown for it, and when the leaders of the community were off basking in pastoral bliss he could be relied upon to do the farm chores.

There is no evidence that Palmer ever espoused Transcendental beliefs, but as an eccentric he was not alone at Fruitlands. Charles Lane, an Englishman and co-founder of the community, was a misogynist, thought women were carnal, advocated celibacy, but married twice and had a number of children by his second wife. Samuel Bower was a nudist whose activities were restricted to nocturnal perambulations, and, as he wore a white covering on some occasions, was the subject of several reports of a ghost flitting about the Fruitlands area. Samuel Larned subsisted for a whole year on crackers alone and ate only apples during the following year. And there was also Abram Wood who declared his individuality by changing his name to Wood Abram. It was on the whole a strange lot, one in which Palmer's principled eccentricities were almost obscured.

A story about Palmer at Fruitlands, however, indicates that he never lost the urge to argue a principle. He began to shovel a path through the snow after a heavy winter storm. The path was a right-of-way across a neighbor's farm, but the farmer insisted on shoveling the snow back onto the path, whereupon Palmer would clear it off again. This procedure lasted all day long, neither man weakening, and would have lasted until the snow melted had not one of the two, as the story goes, sent for Ralph Waldo Emerson to settle the matter.

When the Fruitlands community failed in January of 1844, some six months after it had begun, Palmer took it over and renamed it Freelands. The property was kept by Palmer as a place of refuge for wayfarers and tramps and has since reverted to its original and more famous name. It is operated today as a museum, and, besides being one of the few preservations of its kind, it is a most pleasant and relaxing spot to spend a summer afternoon. The Fruitlands Museums have a collection of memorabilia of Joseph Palmer which includes his diary for the period he was in jail and other manuscripts on which this article is based.

Shortly before his death at Freelands, Palmer wrote the following letter, apparently never delivered, to his son:

I had a shock of numbness soon after I got up this morning which caused me to fall, but I soon recovered so that I got up without much hurt. I am now very comfortable, but for fear I may be worse, or have another shock, I thought best to let you know, so that you may see to things here as soon as you think best, as I don't expect to be able to see to anything, and may not be able to take care of myself.

In his refusal to pay the fine imposed on him, Palmer stood with Alcott, who also refused to pay his taxes; both events predate Thoreau's famous act of civil disobedience. Certainly, the correspondence between the beliefs, interests, and deeds of that period of our history and those of the present cannot escape us. Despite the superficiality and often the inaccuracy of these comparisons, incidents occur which reverberate back over the years and reiterate historical lessons. Such an event, noteworthy here because of its linking of the beard and civil disobedience, was the 1967 release of Leonard Baskin's Thoreau stamp showing a likeness of the Concord author complete with a full beard. The design caused a minor furore: indignant outbursts from some Americans and undoubtedly feelings of "quiet desperation" in others.

Finally, the story of Joseph Palmer is one of those intriguing historical grace notes which tells us much about the social and intellectual climate at a particular point and place in our history. Palmer was a principled man and he could have, but would not, make life easier for himself; he accepted responsibility for his actions when he attempted to redress his grievances and reform the jail at Worcester. His story reveals what it meant to be self-reliant and independent, to run counter to the beliefs of the dominant culture, and to be an individual in a society where most men were followers.

21 June 1812, Sabbath pleasant. at nine oclock attended the funeral of Mrs Brown of Templeton who, without any known cause, put a period to her existance by cutting her throat with a rasor!!! leaving an infant 10 weeks old and a daughter 3 years to the care of a disconsolate husband!—Attended meeting at Templeton in forenoon & returned home at noon as I went, in company with Dr & Mrs Stone, & Mr John Bowker. called at Mr Willingtons at noon where our carriages were left. In afternoon attended our own meeting. Mr Bascoms Text Deut. 82, 29 "Oh that they were wise—that they understood this, that they would consider their latter end." Sung Montague, Canaan, & Greenwich. In forenoon, Chockset, Templeton, & Windham. Mr Willingtons text Job 5, 7 "Yet man is born unto trouble as the sparks fly upward." Sung Windham & 146 psalm tune. Mr Joel Gouldings child baptized Maryann & Mr Josiah Biglows' Sabrina—Mr J. Stockwel, John Bowker & Mrs Jos. Goulding here at noon. Bowker went home before tea.

MS Journal of Ruth
Henshaw Bascom,
American Antiquarian
Society.

Alum Pond and Walden

by Samuel Flagg Bemis

Alum Pond and my boyhood years leave the most vivid and lasting impression of my lifetime, as Walden did with Henry Thoreau. Grandfather had a farm of 145 acres in the town of Sturbridge, Worcester County, Massachusetts. It was situated on the Indian Trail called the Old Bay Path between Massachusetts Bay and Connecticut River, along which the first colonists went out from Boston to Springfield and Longmeadow. It was very close to, or even a piece of the 1000 acres of land west and south of Alum Pond—also called Pookookappog Pond—given in the year 1655 to John Eliot, the "Apostle to the Indians" of early colonial times, by two friendly Nipmuc sachems, Wattaloowekin and Nakin, and confirmed by the Massachusetts House of Representatives in 1715.

Some 100 acres of pasture and second growth stretched between the farm and The Pond, as we always called it. There were three smaller pastures, a meadow, and perhaps twenty acres of arable land for raising corn and hay and fruit and vegetables. Farmhouse, barns, and connecting sheds, all strung together against the rigors of winter, shouldered the Brookfield road about a mile north of the mill village of Fiskdale.

The farm abutted for about a third of a mile on the southern shore of Alum. This beautiful body of water was then an unspoiled Walden. It was better than Walden but it had no Thoreau. The United States Geological Survey enables one to calculate Alum's surface at approximately 225 acres. That is 3.6 times the size of Walden's 62.5 acres. From our southern shore to the point where Thoreau built his "house" on Walden's wooded bank in 46.3 miles as the wild duck wings its way eastward toward the ocean marshes.

Whenever I read *Walden*, which I keep at my bedside, my memories go back to Alum Pond. Hills steeper than those by Walden cupped Alum round about with wood and pastureland. On the west was "Mount" Dan—rising two hundred fifty feet above the Pond. On the then pastured eastern shore there was a fine sandy beach thrown up by the pre-

Samuel Flagg Bemis II, maternal grandfather of Samuel Flagg Bemis III

vailing west wind. Deep springs fed the Pond, as they do Walden, with no substantial brook running into it. The water was clear as an unstained church window. One could see down into it from a boat, some twenty or thirty feet to the bottom, to a lesser depth through clear ice, as Thoreau did at Walden.

A variety of pickerel seemed uniquely indigenous to the Pond, with golden scales quite distinct from those of the greenish denizens that dwelt in Long Pond below, and doubtless a little different from the "great gold and emerald fish" that Thoreau watched at Walden. We caught them in the winter—before the Pond froze too thick to chisel tackle holes—but they did not give up their "watery ghosts" so easily "with a few convulsive quirks," as did those that Thoreau knew; usually they froze stiff only to come to and flop about for some considerable time when they thawed out in the kitchen on the way to the oven of the wood-burning stove. My father once had a basketful of them begin to stir and flop in the heated "steam cars" all the way from Brookfield to Worcester.

The textile company at Fiskdale had secured rights to the water from Alum that flowed through a gatehouse in a brook for half a mile, down under the road to Long Pond. These waters in turn lead into the Quinabaug River that supplied power for the mills. Another smaller body of water called Little Alum, about two miles to the west in the town of Brimfield, also drains into the watershed of the Quinabaug. But don't confuse Little Alum with Big Alum, our Alum.

With no marshy shores or shallow water except for the sandy beach, Alum was not a pond for ducks. But one autumn afternoon, alone and looking down from Mount Dan —I was then about twelve years old —I saw a wondrous sight. A flock of ducks came planing down from the north across the slanting rays of the lowering sun. Then another flock, and another, and another, hundreds and hundreds, thousands came wheeling in battalions circling to

Showing arcade of maple trees planted by S. F. B.'s grandfather, S. F. B. II. Photo dated 1935.

the placid surface for their night's stopover on the way south for the winter. Soon they covered all the northern half of the Pond. The sight almost smothered me as breathless I looked on, and I alone witnessed it, so far as I know. I never beheld so many wild ducks, not even in Canada later, until years afterward I saw thousands wintering in open water by Mount Vernon downstream from the frozen Potomac.

Not unique like the Great Flock of Ducks were the seasonal over-flights of geese north and south: incessantly honking in metallic dissonance and a rapid alternating current of hoarsely clanking gabble until out of hearing. They flew in steady formation, about two hundred yards high, seventy to a hundred in a squadron. I suppose their harsh aerial noise keeps them from losing touch with one another at night or in foul weather. They have no radar, you know. Anyone who has seen or heard wild geese passing over by day or night will never for-

get the sight nor the sure sound they make. I hear the honkers now occasionally in season in New Haven, usually when lying wakeful at night. It so excites me that I used to call to my wife to listen. I like to imagine that the geese have passed over Alum Pond less than an hour ago or will be going over there in a little while.

Why is it that wild ducks in flight don't keep themselves grouped safely by incessant quacking? Perhaps it is because they don't fly in the dark and make only short flights by day. They can't quack very loud, anyway.

At one stretch our shore sloped to the Pond through a lovely grove of young white pines. A carriage trace wound in and out, slalom-like, among the tree trunks, down to the shore. So thick was the carpet of pine needles, and so resilient, that one could scarcely have followed the way for wheeled vehicles were it not for horse droppings. The soft brown groundcover was slick enough to slide on skis from

129

Grandfather and Grand-
mother at the front gate.

the pasture gate at the top of the grove to the pebbly slip where we tied our boats between two boulders. Only we had no skis. I did not know then what skis were. Nobody in our region used them in those days; when the snow was too deep to walk unaided we took to the utilitarian bear-foot snowshoe to get in and out of the woods. In the United States skis are mostly a twentieth-century import. Snowshoes have mostly gone into the New England attics.

When first I saw the Pond, as a child of five or six years, perhaps the year 1896 or 1897, before my parents moved out from Worcester to the farm to take care of my ailing grandfather, there were two little plain-board shacks in the midst of the grove, one room each for sleeping and nothing more; neither cabin big enough to serve even a Thoreau. Down by the shore was a cookhouse, with a screened-in porch, furnished with vertical, board-back benches each side of a long dining table. If one were out in the middle

of the Pond one could not then see any habitation at all—unless it were a bit of the cookhouse in the grove, and the distant Arnold farmstead (long since burned down) on top of the eastern hill. But there was one other little building, a log cabin hidden back in another wood half a mile away on the western shore. It belonged to the "Spencer Boys." They seem to have been the first to discover the idyllic vacation possibilities of Alum Pond. Years later I learned that one of them was Leroy Allston Ames, who became a professor at Clark University, in whose class in American literature I first came to know Thoreau. In after years we talked about Alum Pond. Professor Ames is still living, nearly a hundred years old, in the town of Spencer as I write these lines. He too remembers Alum as a Walden.

It was near the turn of the century that Grandpa Sam built his first real cottage at the Pond—the Dam Cottage, he called it, because it was close to the dam and gatehouse through which the Pond emptied. There was a little beach at this spot. Grandpa let the Baptists use it for their fresh water immersions. He himself was an Adventist, but Grandma was a Baptist.

To the cabins in the grove and the Dam Cottage, Grandpa Sam later added the Middle Cottage and the East Cottage, a hundred yards or more apart, for the purpose of renting them out to summer campers, who were beginning to venture into the hinterland by horse and buggy from Southbridge, or even from Worcester and Springfield by the railroad to Brookfield. About the same time a neighboring farmer who owned an equal or perhaps larger tract north of us, on the west side of the Pond, began to build cottages and rent them out. This was the beginning of a sequence of summer dwellings that now ring the Pond almost side to side on plots little bigger than city houselots. As soon as this phenomenon set in, the cottagers resurrected the old Indian name from early colonial maps and called it Lake Pookookapog. But we continued to call it Alum Pond, and so it appears on the United States Geological Survey Maps of 1946 and 1954. What the origin of this name is I do not know. Maybe alum?

The Pond would have maintained a fairly constant level in dry times as well as in wet seasons, thanks to its everlasting deep and undiscovered springs, but the takings of water to keep the village mills in steady power would sometimes lower the level abruptly. It was a shame to see Alum shrink even a rod from high-water mark. In winter the lowering and rising of the water would strain the frozen surface so as to create great cracks that would shoot quickly here and there, sometimes all across the Pond, the heavy ice rumbling loudly with the torture. One could hear these great groans reverberating like thunder half a mile away at the farmhouse. We boys knew what the noise was all right but sometimes at night it combined with the frosty creaking of the house itself to make us pull the bedclothes over our heads.

Thoreau mentions the booming of winter ice, but his Walden did not groan as loud and mournfully as our suffering Alum; there were no mills in Concord to draw the water off so dreadfully. He explains the booming of Walden ice in terms of changing atmospheric conditions, which doubtless affected Alum Pond too. He also mentions cracks wrought in Walden's frozen shore! I never saw any small earthly fissures by our Pond such as the hermit philosopher observed near his cabin during these winter travails. What would Henry Thoreau have thought of today's sonic booms?

We used to do a bit of fishing through the ice. Good bait was rather hard to get at the farm in the middle of winter. We used native shiners when we could buy them, otherwise "mumechugs." One winter during our life there some city fishermen rented one of our cottages for a few days and set out their lines. They had a great quantity of lively shiners, which they kept in a gunnysack hung with its contents in the water below the ice. After breakfast the second morning one of them went out to cut the ice from that hole to bring up enough shiners for the day's operations. Rather careless with an ax, he severed the rope. That unsteady stroke ended the fishing for this group. They told their sad story to us as they went home. Next day my father went up to the cottage, chopped the hole open, took a long pole and hooked up the sack. The shiners were perfectly lively. He carried them home in a big milk can and put them in the cows' watering trough. We had good live bait all that winter.

In later time, after I went to college, I used to go back to Alum Pond fishing in the winter. I remember one such occasion, with college chums. In the bitter cold the holes froze over faster than we could stir the water to keep them open. But we were catching fairly well. A party of men had set up tackle down the Pond not too far from ours, near a cottage which they

had rented. They were spending most of their time merrily inside, but every once in a while they would delegate someone who had lost a round of cards and who was still sober enough not to fall down and freeze to death, to go out and inspect the lines. He was expected to bring in a fish or pay a fine. But the holes were frozen up so much that it was hopeless. These delegates would make their way over to us boys and buy one of our pickerel. We were in real business before the day was over. Our competitors had something to brag about when they got back to the city, and we were glad to gather in the shekels, with some of our own fish—the biggest— to spare.

Alum Pond was so strongly stamped on my mind that through several years of early adult life I had a recurring dream about it. I would go back to visit it only to find the water very low, the Pond almost dried up, the bare and muddy bottom strewn with rocks and boulders, stagnant pools in earthly hollows disclosed by the vanished waters. Perhaps it meant that this happy environment had passed forever out of my life. At any rate the nightly illusion recurred less frequently when I began to spend summers by mountain, forest, and lake—one of them on our honeymoon in a wild canyon hard by Pike's Peak. By the time we bought a grove and log-cabin of our own on a lovely lake in New Hampshire—now also circled by summer cottages—the dream had disappeared altogether. I had forgotten about it until I began these pages.

Imagine the shock recently when, motoring by the farm, I came upon a fantastic new phenomenon: the Massachusetts Turnpike had been slapped right across our former pasture between the Pond and the farmstead, above the Brookfield Road, surmounting Long Pond on stilts, and over the hills and far away hell-and-gone to the West. Spoiled forever are the unity and charm of the Old Place. The whirring scream of incessant motor traffic can now be heard where once only the farm wagons creaked, before them the echoes of William Pynchon's Puritan pioneers halooing their way through the wilderness toward Connecticut's gleaming water, and long before them the silent pad of Indian moccasins treading the Old Bay Path.

Boyhood years are gone but the memory of Alum Pond lingers on. How good to have had in the nineteenth century—that happiest century in the history of mankind—a peaceful Walden or a tranquil Alum behind the tensions of life in this our tumultuous twentieth century!

"To the Glory of Religion, and the Credit of the Town, there are four Churches, Built with Clap-boards and Shingles, after the Fashion of our Meeting-houses; which are supply'd by four Ministers, to whom some, very justly, have apply'd these Epithets; one a Scholar, the Second a Gentleman, the Third a Dunce, and the Fourth a Clown."

Edward Ward. *A Trip to New-England with a Character of the Country and People, both English and Indians,* London, 1699.

The Ten-Footers of New England

by Ethel A. Hunter

The ten-footers, those small backyard shops where old-time shoemakers plied their trade, no longer echo to the rat-a-tat of their industrious hammers.

But many of the small buildings still remain, of keen interest to tourists, historians, and those who enjoy reliving old ways and days by studying antiques. Some are in museums, like the ones at Old Sturbridge Village, Sturbridge; at the Essex Institute, Salem; at Natick, Rowley, Boxford, Lynn, and other New England communities. Many are now serving as garages or roadside stands. Where the shops were an integral part of the houses, they have become kitchens or garden toolhouses.

Not all were precisely ten-footers. Some were as large as eighteen by twenty-one feet, with perhaps a second story if the owner planned to hire a journeyman shoemaker or to train apprentices. The average size was twelve by fourteen feet; the architecture, easily recognizable, was varied by the placing of the door, windows, and chimney. The roof might be higher pitched than most

if workmen were also to sleep under it. This recourse was often necessary, especially in the earliest days when few itinerant workmen had transportation, and a shoemaker might live miles from a shop. He would sleep on a pallet in the attic, warm his plain meals on the shop stove or eat in his employer's kitchen, then walk home cheerfully when a "run" of work was finished. He planned to have a ten-footer himself someday!

They were snug little buildings, usually set on the south side of the house to shield them from wintry blasts, and under a big shade tree. A rampant trumpet vine or woodbine often climbed over the whole structure.

Inside, the place was redolent of freshly tanned leather that gave off a pungent, acid odor. When burned in the potbellied stove in the form of "jimpins" (waste scraps and skivings of leather), it gave off a still more acrid odor and a mild heat.

The lighting (shoemakers often went to work at six in the morning and worked until eight at night) was done with candles or whale-oil lamps, superseded in later years by

Interior and exterior of the shop owned by the Rowley Historical Society. *Photos courtesy of Everett D. Jewett.*

kerosene lamps set in iron brackets around the walls.

Early shops such as the one at Essex Institute had a simple, low bench with a hollowed-out place where the worker sat. An upright cabinet of drawers to hold tools and materials stood at the end of the bench and the "cabbage box" beneath. This box was a wide, deep drawer where the shoemaker kept scraps of leather too good to burn. Sometimes, by skillful, close cutting, by hammering the leather out thin and stretching it with pincers, the shoemaker could "cabbage out" leather enough to make a pair of shoes for his family's use or to sell.

The benches were called "berths," and the workmen a "crew" in coastal communities. In back-country regions the benches were "letting pews" and the workers a "gang." They made the whole shoe by hand, using the most primitive of tools and materials.

Stitching was done in crude wooden clamps held between the knees. The thread was a 6-, 8-, or 10-strand hemp cord, with a waxed end or hogsbristle for a needle. Sometimes thin sheepskin thongs were used for the "closing," or sewing the uppers, a process immortalized in Lucy Larcom's poem, "Hannah Binding Shoes."

Soles and heels were cut from thick, crumpled cowhide or sheepskin, tanned in a neighborhood bark-pit, softened with mutton tallow, and then hammered smooth on a lapstone. Lasting and bottoming were done on a wooden last, carved from a piece of pine wood and held on the operator's lap with a strap or "stirrup" that went down under his instep.

Soon the ingenious Yankees began to fit out their shops with crude inventions. One of the earliest was a pegging machine that replaced the tedious process of making a row of holes around the sole of a shoe with the awl, then hammering in the pegs one by one.

A crimping machine was contrived to press and cut the front part of the upper into shape, so that it fitted over the toes without pinching. Then, instead of "ragging" the uppers — that is, scrubbing them with a rag or piece of carpet, to make them pliable and glossy — a treeing machine was rigged up to iron and polish them. Steel dies for cutting out shoe parts took the place of paperboard or tin patterns. Now for the first time, about the year 1850, people could have rights and lefts, or "crooked shoes," instead of ugly "straights."

With the invention of the sewing machine in the 1840's, work in the small shops changed. They began to take in work from large central shops, precursors of the modern factory. "Freighters," large covered wagons drawn by a span of horses, peddled stock around the countryside and picked up the finished shoes.

This "put-out work," consisting of precut soles, machine-stitched uppers, and partially finished heels, was easier to work on and also paid better.

The amazing output of the ten-footers is hard to comprehend today. In them the hardy, industrious workers shod the majority of the inhabitants of northeastern United States, also sending their shoes to the Far South and to the West Indies in casks and hogsheads that came back filled with molasses. Pioneers, moving ever westward, carried their skills with them and left on the frontiers an eager market for the solidly crafted shoes of the eastern seaboard.

The owners of the ten-footers were in their day perhaps the most independent fellows in the world. They called no man boss, had few labor troubles, and obeyed no factory whistle. In summer they worked in their gardens and orchards; in fact, many ran good-sized farms, since summer was a "slack" time.

If they were hungry they could nip over to the house for a snack; if tired, they could take off time for a nap or the whole day, for that matter. When weather favored, they painted and repaired their buildings, went to the gristmill with grain, took the horse to the black-

Henry Wilson's shop in Natick.

Interior of Henry Wilson's shop.

smith to be shod (or did this themselves), and seldom missed a chance to go fishing and hunting in season.

These versatile workers often had a highly respected position in local affairs. They were elected to serve as selectmen and on the school board. They sat at their benches working with patient fingers, while according to tradition, they held long philosophical and political discussions with fellow townsmen who respected their opinions.

Benjamin Franklin called them "garret philosophers." Charles Francis Adams once said that when the Civil War broke out the men of Weymouth, Massachusetts, a town where ten-footers dotted the landscape, seemed better posted on national affairs than the men of nearby Quincy. He laid this situation to the fact that the men of Quincy worked in the noisy quarries, where there was no chance for discussion.

The writer of a pamphlet now in the Newburyport Library recorded:

The cordwainers (an early name for shoemakers) often worked while one of their number read aloud from books and newspapers. No class of mechanics are more quietly disposed, give less trouble to their employers, possess a larger fund of general information or grasp the leading questions of the day more readily.

Many were prominent beyond their own locale. There was John Greenleaf Whittier, who as late as 1825 worked at making the family's shoes, as did so many farmers in the long, shut-in hours of winter. This homely toil, along with his other labors on the farm, laid the foundation for his deep interest in and warm sympathy with the industrious workers of the time. His poem, "The Shoemakers," one of his *Songs of Labor*, shows his familiarity with the craft.

Rap! Rap! upon the well-worn stone
How falls the polished hammer.
Rap! Rap! the measured sound has grown
A brisk and merry clamor.
Now shape the sole; now deftly curl
The glossy vamp around it;
And bless the while the bright-eyed girl
Whose gentle fingers bound it.

Henry Wilson, the "Natick Cobbler," learned to make shoes in the ten-footer preserved there in his honor, with much of its crude equipment still intact. This enterprising gentleman, after short but fruitful attempts to further his scant schooling, returned to the shoe business first as a factory worker and then as an owner. He prospered, entered politics, and, like Whittier, became an ardent abolitionist. He went into the State and then the United States Senate, finally becoming the twentieth Vice President of the United States.

He always claimed, as did others, that shoemakers were immensely influential in the abolitionist cause, arguing it hotly in the shops, holding meetings, and building up a strong body of opinion in favor of freeing the slaves.

Children of that era have recorded many interesting stories of those exciting days and other, more engaging, memories too.

One remembered vividly her grandfather, hustling to finish a case of shoes before milking time so that he could, in the long, spring twilight, plant his garden or, in winter, attend a meeting of the Crispins, a shoemakers' union.

Another recalled the littered benches; the many little square boxes filled with hand-cut nails, tacks, and pegs; the balls of yellow wax; the great variety of hammers

The Hiram N. Breed shoe shop in Lynn, now on the grounds of the Lynn Historical Society. *Library of Congress Collections.*

and awls, pincers, nippers and keen knives, some cleverly curved and pointed. Also, with a man's keen interest in tools, he could identify some that are collectors' items today: the spokeshave (a small copy of a wheelwright's tool) ; the edge-setter; the "jigger" (a small notched wheel for marking where the pegs would go) ; the last-puller; the scourer; the shoulder-stick; and the colt.

Of course, almost all the children who hung around the shops learned to make shoes, stitching and pegging valiantly beside their elders. This is not a picture of child labor in its harsher aspects. There were not many amusements in those days, and youngsters were brought up to like and respect work. Most were glad to eke out the family income and proud of their skills.

Then, almost overnight it seemed, the factories, clattering with ma-

he Lye-Tapley Shop, ca. 1830, now on the ounds of the Essex Institue. *Photo courtesy the Essex Institute.*

Children working at shoemaking before the days of factories. *Library of Congress Collections.*

chinery run by steam and then electric power, began to lure away the skilled workers from the ten-footers. At first this was fiercely resented. Among farmers and in small village communities, especially, the shoemakers stuck obstinately to their lasts, tack hammers, and awls in their own convenient shops. They dreaded to see the good craft of shoemaking turned into a machine industry. They feared that machines would become masters of mankind and turn time-honored creative skills into monotonous toil.

But progress is irresistible, especially to so keen and practical a breed as the New England Yankee. It gradually became clear that labor-saving machinery was exactly that, saving of time and energy in a rapidly expanding economy. And since the new machines were too large and too expensive for the small shops, the ten-footers closed, one by one, forever.

Most of them were abandoned to other uses. Today they are picturesque reminders of an independent mode of living, rigorous and demanding, but eminently satisfactory to the workers of yesteryear.

The Blackstone Canal

by Brenton H. Dickson

"We have welded Worcester and Providence together and it will take a stronger arm than that of Samson to break us apart."

So said an enthusiastic supporter of the Blackstone Canal when, after a delay of twenty-four years, it finally got its charter from the Massachusetts Legislature.

The idea of a canal connecting the two cities originated in the late 1700's; in 1796 John Brown of Providence and his associates surveyed a route. A company was incorporated under the laws of Rhode Island—but not in Massachusetts. The very thought of the landlocked treasures of Worcester County finding their way to market by way of Rhode Island, with Providence benefiting from business that rightly belonged to Boston, was unthinkable. Residents of East Greenwich, Rhode Island, were also disturbed. The market for agricultural products, they said, would be glutted with produce grown in and around the Blackstone Valley.

Without a Massachusetts charter, the whole project had to be abandoned and was not revived until the early 1820's. This time a charter was granted. Many Bostonians still dreaded the evil consequences, and only a few months before completion, the Boston *Centinel* issued a stern warning that if it "is not counteracted by some similar enterprise in this town, Boston will be, in a very few years, reduced to a fishing village."

During the years of delay (1796-1820) great changes took place in the Blackstone Valley. Industrial establishments had been quick to recognize the water power potential of the river, with its average drop in altitude of ten feet per mile between Worcester and Providence. Although "a very Tom Thumb of a river, as rivers go in America," according to an article in *Technical World*, investigation by experts showed that "the hardest working river, the one most thoroughly harnessed to the mill wheels of labor in the United States, probably the busiest in the world, is the Blackstone." Expressed in terms of number of factories per mile, this could well be true.

The canal promoters decided first to sound out the sentiment of the mill owners along the line, presenting arguments in favor of a waterway. "A man and a horse," they said, "can move to and from market 20 or 25 tons on a canal [at] three miles an hour, with greater ease than the ordinary wagon loads are moved on the road . . . A vessel on a canal is independent of winds, tides and currents, and is not exposed to the delays attending conveyances by land; and with regard to safety, there can be no competition . . . It costs less to transport a ton of heavy goods from Liverpool across the Atlantick, 3000 miles, to Boston, than from Boston to Worcester by land, a distance of 40 miles . . . However strong habit of business may be, the love of gain is stronger; and whatever may be the force of attachment to old channels of trade, and old methods of intercourse, they will give way to the powerful attraction of making money. The savings will be too great, the lure too enticing to be resisted." And judging from experience on the Middlesex Canal (Boston to Lowell), the land close to the Blackstone was bound to increase greatly in value.

Savings in transporting freight by water was an important factor in winning over the mill owners, although they were apprehensive of an abnormal drain on their water supply. The canal company agreed to build a large reservoir in Sutton to take care of this, but there were other rigid restrictions that could not be so easily dismissed. In Rhode Island, for instance, the legislature prohibited the canal from interfer-ing with the "natural flow of the waters" from sources of the Blackstone River or drawing off water lower than a mark designated by monuments set by the commission-ers. When the canal drew water from the river, it must return an equal amount within an hour. There is some question whether it could be operated at all under these conditions. Filling a lock would require around 5000 cubic feet of water on an average, and when this figure is multiplied by the number of locks (49), and the resulting figure by the number of fillings to accommo-date the heavy traffic anticipated, the necessary cubic footage is fairly substantial.

Surveys, cost estimates, and an estimate of the water supply were completed in 1822. The canal would be forty-five miles long, including navigable portions of the river. It would be thirty-two feet wide at the top, eighteen at the bottom, and three and a half feet deep. Cargo boats, seventy feet long, nine to ten feet wide, and drawing thirty inches when loaded, could pass each other on the stretches between locks. To descend from Worcester to Narra-gansett Bay, 451 feet, would require forty-nine locks. Forty-eight would be made of stone, which was nearly as cheap as wood and much more permanent. The stone would be cut in a granite quarry close to the canal in Northbridge, and, with the canal completed, the quarry could become

The canal going by some mills, c. 1903. *Photo courtesy of the Rhode Island Historical Society.*

a profitable enterprise. "The quarries at Northbridge are of great excellence," according to an article in the *Massachusetts Spy*. Granite is "very abundant almost directly on the banks of the canal, and we understand that considerable quantities are already engaged for the Providence market. From that place it will probably soon find its way to New York, where it may yet come as extensively into use as the Chelmsford and Quincy stone have."

The surveying and engineering is attributed to Benjamin Wright—"a skillful engineer under whose superintendence and estimates, the middle section of that stupendous work, the Erie Canal was constructed." It is believed, however, that most of the work was done by Holmes Hutchinson of Rhode Island. This might partially explain why a fundamental rule of canal building was disregarded in using slack water in the river from time to time instead of confining the canal

to its own ditch. Experience had already demonstrated to DeWitt Clinton and others, the folly of improving a river for navigation and the wisdom of a canal paralleling its banks.

The Blackstone used the river for about a tenth of its distance which involved entering and leaving the river sixteen times, each time drawing water from the reservoir of some manufactory—a situation bound to cause ill feeling and jealousy. In periods of low water, boats would be stranded on the river shoals, while during times of flood the current would be too swift for safe navigation. As a result, the entire length of canal could not be used for days or even weeks at a time, and goods, ready for shipment, must wait for the right conditions. This fact, coupled with the necessity for closing the canal four or five months on account of ice, would cut seriously into profits.

These difficulties were not fore-

A view of the canal, probably in Mass. *Photo courtesy of the Rhode Island Historical Society.*

seen. When the stock was offered for sale in Providence, there was a wild scramble for it; within three hours it was oversubscribed one hundred percent. Messengers were quickly dispatched to Worcester to see if any additional stock could be picked up there, but on arriving they found that the Worcester quota had also been oversubscribed. Those who were left out little realized, at the time, how fortunate they were!

Excavation began in Rhode Island in 1824, and ground was broken in Worcester in July 1826. Five hundred construction workers were employed in Rhode Island, their wages ten to twelve dollars a month exclusive of board. Work progressed slowly, since the digging must all be done with hand tools. Besides, there were the whims of the weather to contend with.

"All through 1827 the work on the Blackstone Canal has been prosecuted with busy industry," said a news item. "The heavy rains of spring and the sudden tempests of autumn have certainly had an unfavorable effect upon the excavation but much less than . . . expected. Some difficulties were experienced by contractors abandoning their section, but in many cases much of such work has been relet advantageously." Then, several months later, "The unusual supply of rain descending in continual showers, has been particularly unfavorable to the progress of the work. The contractors have been delayed in their operations by the fountains and streams bursting from the earth shadowed by constant clouds, and poured down from every hillside." The article goes on to say that reports of damage to canal banks are exaggerated.

The Rhode Island section was completed several months ahead of the Massachusetts, and the directors planned a number of excursions for the sake of publicity. The *Lady Carrington*, a grand and beautiful vessel with "a palatial cabin running most of the length of her body," was built as a passenger boat and completed in Providence June 28, 1828, at a cost of $2500.00. Named for the

The lock at Millville.

wife of Edward Carrington, one of the principal promoters of the canal, she was fitted up in the best style for the accommodation and comfort of her passengers. She was painted white and had red curtains in her windows. On the first day of July she started up the canal from the lock opposite the jail on Canal Street, Providence, on her maiden voyage to Albion Mills, about ten miles away. "A salute of artillary announced her departure, seconded by the cheers of those on board, and the shouts of hundreds of spectators who crowded the banks and surrounding emminences to witness the novel spectacle." There was a band of music aboard of eight or ten pieces, and her departure was witnessed by a large and admiring crowd. Among the select company aboard were "His Excellency the Governor, two of the Rhode Island Canal Commissioners and about fifty citizens. The boat was drawn up the canal by a tow line attached to two horses, that travelled with rapidity on the

straight levels . . . Between tide water and Albion factory, nine granite locks of most substantial masonry were passed . . . The novelty of ascending and descending . . . was particularly gratifying to those who had never before witnessed the operation."

"The party partook of an excellent collation on board the boat furnished by the proprietors . . . It was not merely the sale [sic] and enlivened feeling and good fellowship that prevailed on board the boat . . . which gave to this excursion an interest that rarely attaches to a party of pleasure."

On July 4th the *Lady Carrington* carried an excursion party from Providence to Scott's Pond amid great rejoicing. Somewhere along the way the boat struck the canal bank. A man who was sitting on the railing, telling a story, suddenly went overboard. After he was pulled in, dripping wet, he shook himself off, resumed his position on the railing, remarked "as I was saying," and continued with the story as if nothing had happened.

Construction, or rather digging with picks and shovels and moving the earth with wheelbarrows, continued into the autumn of 1828 on the Massachusetts section of canal. On the 7th of October, the first boat to travel the entire length arrived in the Port of Worcester. Next day the *Lady Carrington* arrived amid great excitement. She moored in the upper basin at 11 o'clock in the forenoon, to the ringing of bells and roaring of canon. Her cargo, according to the press—"Canal Commissioners, Salt and Corn." An address was delivered from the deck of the boat by Colonel Merrick, chairman of the selectmen, after which a large number of invited guests "repaired to the hospitable mansion of the Governor [Lincoln] and partook of a sumptuous collation furnished in his usual hansome style."

The return trip to Providence was less glamorous. The *Lady Carrington,* having disposed of her cargo of dignitaries who returned home over the road, was now loaded with such nondescripts as butter, chairs, paper, and so on.

One item of cargo which the promoters felt was sure to bring in steady and substantial profits was coal mined in Worcester. Professor Hitchcock in his *Geology of Massachusetts* wrote, "Though inferior to the coal of Pennsylvania and Rhode Island, it will be considered by posterity, if not by the present generation, as a treasure of great value. I can hardly believe that a coal which contains probably not less than 90 per centum of carbon should not be employed, in some way or other as a valuable fuel." The coal had, for some time, been converted into a pigment known as Black Lead, which was a cheap and durable covering for roofs and building exteriors. It was also considered suitable for furnaces where "intense heat and great fires are required."

The coal received much publicity in local papers. "Several people have had their stoves fitted for the coal, intending to make constant use of it." In Providence, "The coal from Worcester has been tried in the counting house of Mr. Joseph Manton and approved of." In Worcester, "Captain Thomas has fitted up a stove for burning it in his barroom where for about a week past, he has not used a particle of any other fuel, and has had as handsome and as good a fire as we have ever witnessed of either the Lehigh or the Schuylkil coal." Could this opinion have been influenced by a touch of what Captain Thomas served in his barroom?

The mine was developed by Col. Amos Binney. A shaft was driven three hundred feet into the hill, where at one time twenty men were employed. Expensive machinery was installed, as well as a railroad for bringing out the coal. A track was planned to connect the mine with

The canal near Lincoln, R. I.

the canal basin, where coal could be efficiently loaded onto barges and floated off to market. But when Col. Binney died the mine was closed and "the mineral which might be made to give motion to the wheels of manufacturing . . . has been permitted to rest undisturbed in its bed." Many people who used the coal, publicity notwithstanding, were inclined to feel it was vastly overrated. One user caustically remarked that the residual ash weighed more than the coal itself!

The arrival of the first boat in Worcester did not mean inauguration of regular service; there was still much to be done before the canal could be considered complete. On November 8th, however, boats began making regular trips and on that day a fleet of six boats arrived in Worcester from Providence. A few days later the *Massachusetts Spy* announced that "a quantity of cherry plank and joist was landed in this town . . . which grew in Michigan or

Ohio at the head of Lake Erie, from whence it was shipped down the lake to Buffalo thence by the Erie Canal to Albany, from that place to Providence by sloop navigation and from Providence to this place by the Blackstone Canal, a distance . . . of at least 900 miles, four hundred of which is artificial navigation. It is thus that articles are made valuable in one section of the country where otherwise there would be no market for them, and another section is supplied at a fair rate with that which it must otherwise do without or buy at . . . exorbitant prices."

The canal had not long been in operation before boatmen discovered that short hauls were much more profitable than long ones, especially in sections with fewer locks. Since the heaviest locking was north of the Rhode Island border, service to Worcester began to suffer. As early as December 1828, only one month after the canal had opened, the *Massachusetts Spy* observed that the inhabitants of the terminal city "have derived but little benefit from the open state of the canal during the mild weather of the last fortnight, although they had hundreds of tons of freight that they were anxious to get up. The reason is that all the boats now on the canal can be more profitably employed in doing the business of the lower end of the route. We hope our citizens will take measures to have a regular line of boats from this place early in the spring." This situation was never satisfactorily remedied; the canal had so many items working against it that more reliable shipping methods were favored.

Potential passengers, faced with taking the fourteen-hour trip from Worcester to Providence by boat, with possibly an overnight stop either at a tavern along the way or using the indifferent sleeping accommodations aboard, preferred the stagecoach which left at eight o'clock in the morning and arrived at five o'clock in the afternoon. The boat served its purpose, however, in taking passengers on pleasure jaunts —it was "a pleasant and comfortable conveyance for invalids who desire to travel or to take the sea air." Special excursion rates were advertised in the autumn when Brown University held commencement exercises—or when the Friends Yearly Meeting was held at Newport.

One of the better remembered excursions was from Uxbridge to Waterford, where the Congregational Society played host to the Uxbridge Congregational Society. "So together with many from North Uxbridge they made a goodly number. They went by canal. The boat was decorated with festoons and evergreens and . . . a kind of bannerette . . . called Gideon's Lamp." The trip took three hours; at times progress was so slow that many of the passengers got out and walked. At one sharp turn the boat nearly upset. When they got to the picnic spot there was a scarcity of food due to a misunderstanding—guests from Uxbridge expected their Waterford hosts to provide the meal, but the Waterford people had no such intention—it was to be "Dutch treat," they said. Things looked gloomy for the Uxbridge guests until a Mr. William Capron came to the rescue with a barrel of crackers and a quantity of cheese. Out of this, the Uxbridge people made their lunch and didn't have to go away hungry.

In the second year of operation occurred the first instance of sabotage on the canal. The embankment of a feeder near Millbury was destroyed by some laborers in the employ of a manufacturing establishment. The incident received much adverse publicity and the embarrassed mill owner, who had ordered the work done, made reparation. As time went on, sabotage became less and less of a transgression. There were constant disputes between

147

The canal terminal at Providence. *Photo courtesy of the Rhode Island Historical Society.*

boatmen and millowners. The mill owners said the canal was using too much water. The boatmen maintained, correctly, that there wouldn't be all that water there except for the reservoirs built by the canal company. In order to conserve the dwindling water supply, mill owners dumped large stones and other refuse into the locks during the night to render them inoperative. Boatmen retaliated by threatening to burn the mills, and armed guards had to be hired as a precaution.

In spite of all this, the canal proved beneficial to the mill owners. An impetus was given to production and trade and factories on the river nearly doubled, which, unfortunately, the water supply did not. In the year 1830 alone, 1000 new people settled in Millbury. Worcester became the largest city in the county—it had ranked only fourth before the canal was built and it was soon "the center of a more extensive trade. Mechanical and manufacturing enterprises came into existence, and the way was prepared for Worcester to become the center of a great network of railroads." The whole line of canal "remains richer and more populous in consequence of its brief existence."

The canal also had its romantic side. "On pleasant evenings all along the shore were many . . . trysting places for young men and maidens. The banks . . . formed a very agreeable promenade and it was made the most of too." On moonlight nights "the almost motionless water was well covered by rowboats, for the lovers of those days found upstream trips under the overhanging trees highly romantic." Swimming was enjoyed in the canal during the summer months, while in winter the long flat stretches were ideal for skating.

On the less pleasant side, large wharf rats from Rhode Island arrived on the boats and eventually became the curse of nearly all the inhabitants living in the vicinity of the canal.

Boston merchants were continually bemoaning the loss of business to Providence. Heavy goods from New York that had formerly been shipped overland from Boston, now reached Worcester by way of the canal or by a combination of canal and team. Even in winter this freight bypassed the capital city, when the canal horses were used for hauling freight along the roads of the Blackstone Valley.

This undesirable situation was short-lived. The era of the railroad was fast approaching to sound the death knell of New England canals. In 1831, only three years after the Blackstone started operating, the Boston and Worcester Railroad was incorporated, the enacted bills being signed by Leverett Saltonstall as President of the House of Representatives. Capital for the road was raised mostly in Boston and its vicinity. Few investors could be found in Worcester. They had already lost money on the Worcester Turnpike and the Blackstone Canal, and they weren't going to be burned again. Even though existing traffic figures showed great potential for a railroad, they were not enough to convince the skeptical Worcester investor.

The Boston and Worcester became, almost immediately, a highly successful enterprise. Canal tonnage went into a sharp decline. A railroad from Worcester to Providence was soon in the works, and when it was completed in 1844 the canal was dealt a fatal blow. The lingering death that had overhung it, almost since its start, was at last becoming a reality. The hopelessness of the situation had been recognized for some time, a petition for abandonment having been filed in 1841. Other such petitions were filed in 1844, 1846, and 1847 but not granted until 1849, two years after the railroad went into operation and a year after

the last boat had traveled the full length of the canal. A speedy granting had been prevented by a group of manufacturers along the line who argued that the canal corporation should not be allowed to abandon its property until it had compensated mill owners who claimed they had "public spiritedly allowed the company to preempt their water rights." According to memorials to the General Assembly for 1841, millowners "would further state that they have been constantly harassed by this [canal] corporation ever since they were permitted to enter the river; — that they have been at great expense and trouble to protect their property."

In 1837 several judgments had been found against the canal in suits brought by the mills. Total damages amounted to $8,450—nearly as much as tolls for the year—all this despite the fact that the mills were drawing heavily from the canal's reservoirs.

These troubles could hardly have been avoided unless the canal had control over the water rights. As it was, it had merely secured joint use. Had it been dug twenty-five years earlier and confined to its own ditch, it probably would have been a lucrative enterprise even after the advent of the railroad. By owning water rights on the river and selling power to the mills, it could have continued prosperous although the form of transportation had become outmoded.

Tolls reached their peak in 1832, three years before completion of the Boston and Worcester Railroad. That year nearly $19,000 was collected—a rather puny figure considering that the canal had cost $750,000 to build. The first and largest dividend was also paid that year—$1.00 a share. During the canal's brief existence total per-share dividends amounted to only $2.75. Stockholders had the compensating privilege of subscribing to stock in the Blackstone Canal Bank.

When the Worcester and Providence Railroad was completed, a passenger could travel between the two cities in two hours. Moreover, the railroad could operate at night, a comparatively recent innovation. Thirteen years earlier, when the Boston and Worcester began operating, night traveling was not permitted unless unavoidable, since the locomotives had no headlights. On one occasion a train got delayed outside Worcester and had to complete its journey after dark. The engineer reported, "ran into some cattle at 9 P.M. and killed two of them. It was so dark, could not see."

When the canal was abandoned, some sections were put to use as water power canals for factories. The locks were dismantled and the blocks of granite, in great demand as foundations of buildings, were sold. Today, the only lock remaining is in Millville. Its stonework is nearly intact. Here can be seen a fine example of the skill that went into nineteenth-century stone cutting. Remains of the old ditch can still be found at a number of places, and in Pawtucket, Rhode Island, several miles where there is still water in the channel are being preserved as a recreational area. Such is the present status of what was once termed *a magnificent enterprise* and at another time *the greatest financial fiasco in the history of Providence.*

The Ubiquitous Mill House: Yesterday Reincarnated

by Ray Young

Just as the medieval castle dominated its village in old England, so did New England's burgeoning textile mills overshadow their towns. But while most of the mills have shut down or vanished, the mill house not only remains, but is staging a comeback. People are looking at it as a well-built home and sometimes even as a status symbol.

The mill house was once roundly condemned as "drab" or "jerry-built," but it was better constructed than many modern development homes, and served as a model for ordinary workers' dwellings in the towns. Now, like the Cape or saltbox, it recalls a time that was less complicated if sometimes more grim.

The mill settlements one still sees scattered through New England were in a sense the first intentional "developments" in this country. They didn't grow with the town, but went where the mill was. If the plant was built near a waterfall, the houses were there, too. If the mill ran along a river, so did the houses. In the days when "shoeleather express" was the working man's transportation, the mill house system was the most practical way to bring the employee to the job. When the bells rang in the mill towers at six a.m., the husband, possibly his wife, as well as some of the children, merely walked up, down, or across the street.

In some towns the mill settlements were "across the tracks," but in more rural settings they were practically independent communities. "Pequot" and "Palmertown" are still the common names for sections of the township of Montville, Connecticut, named after two old mills on the Oxoboxo River. This story is repeated in New England wherever waterfalls, harbors, or rail junctions attracted factories.

"Varietyville," just outside Westerly, Rhode Island, is a typical site that also shows mill house evolution. The settlement is surrounded by overgrown fields, some now wooded, looking as if a giant had picked up a cluster of toy houses and dropped them there. Across the road from the old mill site and a shady grove at the dam is a group of small cottages. Behind the cottages, built somewhat later, are duplexes

151

Modern duplexes in Paw-catuck, Connecticut.

and finally tenements, showing the trend away from houses built for the original Yankee hands to dormitories for French-Canadian and European employees.

The first mill houses kept fairly closely to the old Cape style, built mostly of wood, but sometimes (as around Webster, Massachusetts) of the same stone or brick used for the mill itself. These houses were often equal or superior to the dwellings the mill hands had come from. That cellar hole one may see out in the woods is likely a monument to a conflagration. The practice of anchoring rafters to the central chimney in a Cape farmhouse may have added strength, but it also could be a fire hazard. And contrary to folklore, not all farmers who built Capes out in the country were good carpenters. A main problem with the evolving mill house, on the other hand, was that like any mass-produced item, it was plain in appearance and looked "common." But it was often warmer than nearby farmhouses.

As mills multiplied, the first frame duplex appeared, usually divided into two halves, each with a downstairs and upstairs. Some early duplexes retained the Cape feature of a low upstairs floor with slanted ceilings, while others had full-sized rooms and a walk-up attic. This latter type came along after stoves had become the method of home heating and the old central fireplace—inefficient and a heat drain—had vanished.

Wauregan, Connecticut, a few miles north of Varietyville, shows a classic case of mill-inspired village development. On the north, the motorist enters the town abruptly from the woods and passes a school and weatherbeaten church. Then comes a hillside packed with large white houses, extending almost down to the river. Then appears the mill site, and one is back in the woods again. The whole village was built for the old Wauregan Mills. There, the company economized by putting up double duplexes: long, two-story

Rural tenements, the final evolution of the mill house in country districts.

frame houses broken up into four two-story units. These houses were built for utility; the upstairs windows are considerably smaller than those downstairs, recalling the days when people used bedrooms for sleeping only and spent their waking hours downstairs. The two end apartments had the advantage in summer because they were exposed on three sides. In winter the interior units benefited from the heat of their outside neighbors.

A similar arrangement, on a more elaborate scale, appears in the old houses of the Amoskeag Mills in Manchester, New Hampshire, a place once famed for the manufacture of woolens and steam fire engines. The houses, all of brick, sit across the mill yard from the factories, and extend uphill, each structure's end connected to its neighbors. (This placement results in each front doorstep being about two feet above or below the next one.)

It must have been a rather drab neighborhood. The area was one great mass of brick architecture. The Amoskeag Mills, imposing as they were in all their red turreted glory, blocked off any view of the turbulent Merrimack rapids and were a constant reminder of the next day's work to employees who sat at their windows or on the front doorstep smoking their clay pipes or black cheroots.

But, these rowhouses, being only a block or so from Manchester's main business district, are now coming back into demand as doctors', lawyers', and other professional offices, or as small shops or restaurants. The section was considered an eyesore back when Victorian styling was in eclipse but is now being preserved for its historical value as well as the utility of the houses. And there was no nonsense about construction. Those brick edifices were built to last, just as the mills were intended to provide a perpetual fortune to their owners. It didn't

153

work out the way it was planned for the mills, but the houses remain solid reinforced brick on granite foundations.

Down in Stonington, Connecticut, close to the Rhode Island border, exurbanites from New York have been buying into a row of houses on the harbor. They don't realize that those "quaint sea captains' houses" were originally built as rentals for Portuguese immigrants hired to work in a local machine shop. In nearby Mystic, the road near the famous Seaport abounds in frame houses that sprang up as residences for velvet weavers in a nearby mill—and now are becoming summer homes or gift shops.

"Hallville," a section of nearby Preston, Connecticut, comprises a row of frame houses facing a quiet country road, across from a lily-covered, tree-lined pond formed by the dam of an ivy-covered mill. One of the houses for years had a store front bearing the sign "Hallville Tavern," but the swinging era of mill workers enjoying payday evening draught has given way to that of quiet enclave near to, yet removed from, busy Route 2.

The peace and quiet surrounding many mill settlements today contrasts greatly with the bustle of yesteryear and may be a reminder to those decrying the end of the "good old days." For one thing, the mill house was built for large families in a day when people needed, wanted, and expected less. The kitchen and front room (parlor) tended to be fairly large, while the bedrooms were small and often slept several individuals. But while the smaller duplexes or single-family dwellings were then often crowded, they have ample space for today's smaller family.

Not that space was a great problem in settlements where the mill worked around the clock, because not everyone was home at the same time. Until the First World War in most places, and for years later in some sections, the usual mill day was ten to thirteen hours. This writer's grandfather and three uncles worked in a small Connecticut paper mill on alternating shifts. One week they worked thirteen hours a day from six a.m. to seven p.m. The next, they worked an eleven-hour night trick, from seven to six. Five aunts started in the mill's box factory when they reached age fourteen. Grandma? She had the big kitchen all to herself, getting ready for dinner and supper when the tribe walked home from work.

How well the mill house dwellers enjoyed their community life often depended on the size of the mill. Large developments resembled army camps or were ordinary city neighborhoods. Smaller mills, often out in the country, put up only a

One of the most common examples of nineteenth-century mill architecture, Westerly, Rhode Island.

few houses, usually with plenty of space nearby if not in the front yards. These houses are among the more popular today because of their setting. My family, like many others, preferred to work in a small plant because of the lack of crowding. (This was particularly abrasive to people moving in from isolated country spots in the early mill days and to many industrialized farmers—like my immediate ancestors —as late as the 1920's.) But if the work day was long and the chance of encountering obnoxious neighbors was greater, Sunday was free, and there was no livestock to be tended.

Problems with one's neighbors depended on circumstances, as in any modern development. There was friction between Yankee mill hands and French Canadians in some places, but there was also considerable amalgamation, as around Laconia, New Hampshire, where a large proportion of people with English surnames can claim at least one French ancestor. Later, in the larger cities, mill houses tended to attract colonies of different nationalities as immigration provided a higher percentage of mill hands.

But before you start thinking about "ghettos" and all that, remember that most mill houses that deteriorated did so *after* the mills themselves had declined. The owners, who usually rented them for a low figure such as $10 a month, kept them in repair and expected the occupants to cooperate. The rural slums, the broken-windowed, broken-sided, door-askew wrecks visible today, got that way later.

To the modern homeowner, there are contradictions in mill houses. The structures were made for durability, but not necessarily appearance. Still many reflect a builder who put ornamentation or "gingerbread" or scrollwork on the front because that was the way it

A representative duplex, latter half of the nineteenth century, Varietyville, Rhode Island.

was done. Others reflected the architecture of the mills, and some contrasted with it. The brick or stone mills themselves often abounded in bell towers, steeples, clocks, gingerbread, or at least brick castellation, no doubt because the owners thought that the source of riches should look the part. This didn't always extend to the houses, which were containers for expendable, replaceable, and plentiful help.

Yet the plain mill house was also quite durable. A two-by-four was just that—not the name for a piece of wood an inch-and-a-half by three. Sills were solid beams, not "plates" formed by nailing layers of planks together. And while carpenters had stopped using wood peg construction (that has kept some barns and houses tight for three centuries), they had not yet learned the cost-cutting ways to today's flimsiness. The man shingling a roof was paid two dollars a day for his twelve

hours up there and was expected to leave a tight, weatherproof surface when he finally came down. Foundations were often granite block or brick, mortared tightly enough to be dry even today.

The absence of frills had its drawbacks for the occupant, just as it saved the builder money. For one thing, few mill houses were built for central heating. They had stoves. (This may not be a bad idea today, considering the fuel shortage. The old stove holes are still there under the wallpaper.) Many cellars were low or small, not because people were shorter in those days, but because there wasn't that much need to go below.

Two other drawbacks are lack of insulation and an inadequate electrical system. Insulation wasn't essential back when Gramp, Grandma, Uncle Bill, and the children had quilts or comforters in the bedroom. The kitchen stove was used year round. In winter it heated the house well enough for people who wore woolen underwear and heavy flannels indoors. In summer an insulated kitchen that trapped the heat of the stove would have been unbearably hot.

Mill-house wiring, particularly in northern New England where population has remained static or has declined with the decay of some company towns, is often the old fabric-covered type connected to porcelain pegs. The double push-button wall switch of the 1920's abounds in houses that have wall or ceiling fixtures. Most mill houses out in the country were built in the era of oil or kerosene lamps, so electrification often is a patch-work job. You can tell this by noting the floor plugs in downstairs rooms. It was simpler, quicker, and cheaper to put in these fixtures rather than go into the wall or ceiling. (But many houses with no permanent lights downstairs do have them upstairs, because it was comparatively easy to go through the attic floor to the bedroom or upstairs hall ceiling.)

In Gramp's day the lights, a radio, a washing machine, and toaster made up the peak load on a circuit. Mill owners had to keep up with changing living habits, but they didn't see any sense in going too far. (Even in the 1920's, blown fuses were common.)

Plumbing, even when up to date, still involves some hazards. One of this writer's earliest memories, about 1933, concerns falling into a cess-pool behind a mill house, after stepping on the buried—and rotten —wooden top. So it's often a good idea to watch where you are walking in mill-house yards. Also, most of the old cesspools were merely sumps for waste water from the kitchen sink. (Or, nowadays, dry wells to lessen the load on the newfangled septic tank.)

Some settlements near rivers had sewers. Most rural mill houses, and some urban ones, relied on the little structure out back. Today there are some very large bathrooms in mill houses, arising from conversion of a bedroom. The presence of an extra lavatory in a small room doesn't mean early affluence; it only means that someone decided to convert a closet before deciding to convert bedroom into bath.

Many mill houses have the plumbing pipes fully exposed on the inside wall. This practice, sometimes seen in early mansions, was to keep the pipes from freezing. It's a feature nowadays of some summer homes, where the temperature is kept at a bare minimum in winter when the house is unoccupied.

Some tradesmen, including older ones who once worked as maintenance men in defunct mills, have found a gold mine in mill houses fixed up by city dwellers. Early piping was almost exclusively lead or copper, which were easily worked. So if you renovate, it's a good idea to keep or get credit for any scrap metal that's ripped out, rather than let someone lug it to the junkyard.

This change of junk to treasure symbolizes the way the mill house has been coming out of disrepute in the past ten years, especially since some of the old industrial sites stuck out in the middle of nowhere are now becoming residential. Two main objections to these sites in the past were the now-stilled racket from clattering looms and the coal dust from the mill's powerhouse. These—to the delight of ladies remembering them—are now gone. So, as with many other antiques, prices for mill houses depend on the growing number of people who have heard about them.

"Education in the common sense I had next to none, but there was much chance seed dropped in the fresh furrow, and some of it was good seed, and some of it, I may say, fell on good ground. My father was absorbed in political life, but his affections were at home. My mother's life was eaten up with calamitous sicknesses. My sisters were just at that period when girls' eyes are dazzled with their own glowing future. I had constantly before me examples of goodness, and from all sides admonitions to virture, but no regular instruction. I went to the district schools, or, if any other school a little more select or better chanced, I went to that. But no one dictated my studies or overlooked my progress. I remember feeling an intense ambition to be at the head of my class, and generally being there. Our minds were not weakened by too much study; reading, spelling, and Dwight's Geography were the only paths of knowledge into which we were led. Yes, I did go in a slovenly way through the first four rules of arithmetic, and learned the names of the several parts of speech, and could parse glibly. But my life in Stockbridge was a most happy one. I enjoyed unrestrained the pleasures of a rural childhood."

M.E. Dewey, *Life and Letters of Catharine M. Sedgwick* (N.Y., 1872), pp. 43-4.

The River Gods

THEIR STORY IN WESTERN MASSACHUSETTS
by Elisabeth Linscott

Bill Cummins, who in the early 1800's made his headquarters in Greenfield, Massachusetts, during the busy season on the Connecticut River, was a River God. He was so strong that he could lift a large barrel of salt with one hand by putting two fingers in the bung hole, and, still with one hand, move it from the bottom timbers of his river boat to the top of the mastboard.

Captain Jonathan Kentfield of Sunderland, who passed out rum to his crew when his boat carried the body of a dead Congressman, was a River God, and so was "Sol" Caswell of Gill, who was such an ugly baby that his mother borrowed a neighbor's when she went to quilting bees.

The historians disagree (as historians do) as to when and why this glamorous title was first used. Before the railroad, almost all supplies for the towns from Hartford, Connecticut, to White River, Vermont, were transported on the Connecticut River in flat-bottom boats. The cargoes going upstream included rum, molasses, and mackerel. Downstream came the products of the localities— lumber, brooms, hops, and potash.

When there was no wind, the boats, weighing from thirty to sixty tons, were pushed through the water by the rivermen with long poles. (When the wind blew upstream, the boats sailed easily.) The poles, made of the best white ash, were from twelve to twenty feet long, and two inches or more in diameter, with a socket spike in the lower end and a head on the upper end for the boatman's shoulder. The spiked end was placed firmly on the river bottom and the boatman walked down the side of the boat as it moved forward in the water. With shoulder against the top of the pole, he literally shoved the heavy boat ahead.

Sometimes in swift water or when the boats had to be pushed over bars, five or six men would work on each side, lifting their poles over each other as they took their "sets" on the river bottom. Early authors using extravagant language and writing with awe of the strength of these men, called them River Gods. One author said that poling the boats was "the hardest work ever known to man."

159

Before the canals were built, pilots were necessary to take boats over the falls at Enfield, Connecticut, and Willimansett, and "fallsmen" waited at the foot of the falls to assist in poling boats carrying six to eight tons over the falls.

The pilots were summoned with a signal from the boats. They came running to the shore and often drew lots for the work that paid a dollar and a half for each laborious job.

When the canals were built around the falls, ox teams on shore were used to draw the boats to the locks. Because of the rocky shore, the South Hadley Canal was begun a half mile below the beginning of "quickwater." At high water, it sometimes required fifteen to twenty men to get a boat out of the head of the canal and back into the river. They went ashore with a long track-line hitched to the mast, and, with yokes or collars over their shoulders, trudged and clambered along the bank, with the "polesmen" helping from the boat.

The boatmen were giants, physically hard and tough, but they almost always had bloody shoulders from the friction of the poles, especially in the early part of the season. They tried one thing and another to heal and harden their shoulders, and finally they tried a bit of the cargo they carried—good dark rum. The rum worked better than anything else, so, as one writer recounts: "Every night they opened some rum, put just a little on their shoulders and drank the rest."

Men on the flat-bottom boats whose owners were stingy with rum devised a novel way to get their daily rations. They took a bottle of water and inserted its nozzle in the bung-hole of a full barrel or hogshead of rum. The water, being of heavier specific gravity than the rum, would descend into the barrel, and the rum would consequently be forced up into the bottle.

It was "Sol" Caswell of Gill who told the story about being such an ugly baby that his mother borrowed a neighbor's when she went calling.

When Middlefield's physician and civic leader, Dr. Amber A. Starbuck, was ready to graduate from High School in 1910, she had to prepare an "oration." For her paper she decided to use an interview with old "Sol," one of the last boatmen, who was then eighty-eight. "Sol" went to school only one day in his life.

Here are some excerpts from the interview: "I built my house on this side of the river, on the sand. Lived there 'leven years, then I thought I'd move, so I built a house on t'other side of the river, on the rocks, 'cording to Scriptures ye know, and then in less'n a year, danged if the whole thing didn't go and burn down.

"Well, when I ought to been to meetin', I war jest a'wading out in that river so I knew where every rock lay. You know anybody can steer clear of the rocks that are above the water jest as much as they'd steer clear of a tree on the side of the water, but them that's under water and that the water runs over jest as pretty as ye please, that's what ye have to know and look out for.

"One day jest after the fourteen foot dam had gone out, Lon Gale came from up north with a lot of lumber. All the water way back here went down, when the dam went, but it left all them rocks jest below the surface of the water. They couldn't find anyone who dared to take rafts through French King.* I knew if I did, I would make my name.

"Out of all the Swiftwatermen it took to get the lumber here, only one would go down with me. So I put him in the stern, and when we war a'coming through the 'Horse-race' and almost on to Hog Hole, which was a large eddy, all the Swiftwatermen came down to the river to see me drown, but I'd no idee of doing such a thing, for them's as knows nothing, fears nothing. I turned the raft around and struck the eddy broadside. Jest then the man I had with me put in his oar; the oar jest come up and tossed him eight feet in the air. We never saw that man after he struck the water.

*French King rapids above the mouth of Millers River. Near there now is the French King Bridge on Route 2 near Greenfield.

The River near Mt. Sugar-loaf today. *Photo courtesy of Massachusetts Department of Commerce.*

"The water swept over the raft and struck that left ear of mine and I never heard a thing out of it since, but I hear more than I want to a good many times out t'other one. Howsomever, I knew we were safe for the current took us right out in the middle of the river. After losing one man, I couldn't get another to run with the other five boxes (the rafts). Finally I thought of a man who lived out on the plains. I knew he'd jest as soon be drowned, and I jest as soon he would be, for he was more'n half Indian, so I went and found him. When I told him what I wanted he said, 'Lans, yes, I jest as soon go over the Niagra Falls, if you was at the bow.' He run with me for three days, got every one of them boxes through and never got as much as the sole of his boot wet.

"Them days are gone and the boats, nice ones too, that use to run up and down the river. Some of them cost over seven hundred dollars. Those boats were all left in Hadley locks to jest rot. All 'cause of them railroads coming.

"And now the canal is all grown over with grass, and that electric road runs 'long side of it."

Amber's "paper" included Sol's own account of falling off the dam at Turners Falls:

"That fourteen foot dam had gone out; we were repairing it. I was standing on the first check a'trying to pull a log up, when I slipped jest head first into the check. I knew better than to try and look up, for if I did, I'd strike a check. I kept a'going and a'going. I thought it was the longest dam I ever saw, for I couldn't see light, but you can't see through the bubblers in boiling water. When they saw me, I was eight rods below the dam. Master Hale cried, 'There the rascal is, there he is, but he'll drown going over Fall River Bar.' That was years before he jined the church, so I never laid it up again him.

"Well they started for me, with a boat and grapping hook. I saw them, so I jest filled my mouth with water and spouted it.

"Master Hale saw me and cried, 'He lives for he spouts like a whale, and ye know a man that's drowning can't do that.' After I swum over on to the little peaked island, I went back to the dam and sat down, for I was a little tired.

"Humes had gone over the office and the President of the Company, Mr. Thayer, came over to see if it was true that I did go through the dam. When he saw me, he asked, 'What were you a'thinking of when you were a'going?' 'Well,' I said, 'if I hadn't been more'n half-witted, I'd stopped and picked up them tools you've been a'scolding us for a'losing.'"

Capt. Jonathan Kentfield of Sunderland was one of the early workers on the River, and ran a line of boats on his own account for a number of years. He was very pompous, but was considered a trusty and competent boatman. Once the body of a deceased member of Congress from Vermont was sent home from Washington. It came from New York to Hartford by steamboat, to go by first boat up the Connecticut River. None of the up-River companies were willing to take it. Finally, a man who knew how to handle the Captain told him that the remains had been forwarded to his special care, to go up by his boat.

"Very well," said Captain Kentfield. "Drop down the boat to the steamboat, and take the body aboard! How the people of the city of Washington knew that I was an old and experienced boatman, God only knows." But the men were nervous, so they all took frequent drinks of rum during the night. The story goes that towards morning the Captain called his men and said, "Come aft, men, come aft, and take something to drink; dead bodies aboard —ten or fifteen, maybe; one sartain —and who knows what they died of, perhaps some spontaneous disease? Drink behind that hogshead, and don't for God's sake, let Gen. Culver see you!"

"No business of this country offered so wide a scope of incident and called into action so great a body of jolly, hardworking, determined and unselfish men as that of Connecticut River boating," wrote a Philadelphia historian. "The boatmen were the stoutest, heartiest and merriest of all the men in the Valley."

The strength of these men was so well known that the constables in the cities often called them in to help stop disturbances, and the names of Bill Cummins, Sam Granger, Tim Richardson, and others would "strike terror in the hearts of all loafers, beats or bruisers in the city of Hartford or wherever they were known." Rivermen worked from daylight to dark, had five meals a day, and the Valley rang with their songs. Captain Jonathan Smith of South Hadley and Harlow Humes of Montague were among the well-known singers.

They were expert handlers of boats, masters of the transportation of that period. No one knows who first called them River Gods, but the term suited them. They seemed superhuman!

HOW THE BOATS WERE MADE

The flat-bottom boats of the late eighteenth century were of two classes: oak boats and pine boats. The pine boats were of twenty tons or under, were not very substantially built, and often were sold for lumber at the conclusion of a trip. The oak boats were strongly built of two-inch oak planks, and had a cabin with bunks for the crew. These boats were about seventy-five feet long, fourteen feet wide at the mast, and ten at the stern, with a capacity of thirty-five

to forty tons. They were rigged with a mast about twenty-five feet high, which stood about twenty-five feet from the bow, with shifting shroud and forestays, and a top mast to run up at need. These supported a square mainsail thirty by eighteen feet, and a topsail twenty-four by twelve. They had no keel. The pine boats had neither keel nor rudder and were steered by a long plank set on edge between two pins.

The floor of the oak boat rose gradually from the mast to the bow. From the mast aft to the cabin, it was level, with a gradual rise to the stern. In the pine boats, and sometimes in the oak boats, the space before the mast was open, and the central part used for heavy freight not injured by the weather. The sides were reserved for the operations of the boatmen in rowing and poling.

There were two pairs of rowlocks; and oars were used to aid the current in getting the craft downstream, but were of little use in going upstream. Unless there was a south wind, nothing availed much but the "white ash breeze" [being pushed by the poles of white ash]. The construction and management of these boats are examples of Yankee ingenuity.

The Moonlight Murders on the Isles of Shoals

by Howard W. Muller

A murder rarely has a setting worthy of the horror of the deed. Murders usually take place in surroundings that are mean, sordid, or merely commonplace.

Sometimes there's an exception, like one that happened a hundred years ago on a lonely island off the New England coast. The crime was a fearsome thing to those concerned, though utterly forgotten today. But it took place in a setting worthy of classic tragedy: a hauntingly appealing little bit of American territory, as interesting a place as you'll find anywhere.

The Isles of Shoals are a group of barren rocks six miles off the coast of New Hampshire. From ashore they appear as dim shapes on the horizon, vanishing into the haze. No two are alike.

Duck Island is a dangerous ledge surrounded by half-submerged reefs over which in rough weather the sea spouts and roars. In the olden days it was a death trap of shipping. The prosaic *United States Coastal Survey* for 1854 states grimly, "Vessels approaching Portsmouth from east of the Isles of Shoals should give Duck Island a berth of at least a mile."

Appledore, largest of the group, is a four-hundred-acre chunk of granite and felspar crisscrossed by weird-looking dikes of traprock. It is the site of one of the earliest towns of New England, long since vanished.

Star Island is high and rounded. It is about the size and type of a small, gone-to-seed New England farm, covered with coarse grass through which peep flat boulder tops, and sloping away on all sides to a surrounding rim of black rock. On it are an antique church, a mouldering graveyard, and a summer hotel.

White Island presents a startling contrast to a general picture of austerity. It has a tall, graceful, and beautiful lighthouse, from the top of which in fine weather you can gaze across a whitecapped ocean toward the distant peaks of the White Mountains.

The island of Smutty Nose, where the tragedy took place, is long, narrow, and low-lying, green with vegetation and white with quartz. It stretches away half a mile to seaward and terminates abruptly in a blunt and rather sinister-looking black cape from which the Island takes its name. Take a walk down Smutty Nose if you don't mind roughing it.

Don't be fooled by the deceptively mellow atmosphere, the sweet scents of a New England meadow. The terrain is brutal. You claw your way through waist-high thorn bushes, stumble into crevices in the rock, and are likely at any moment to break your neck falling into some abandoned quarry, or perhaps into the foundation of a vanished house of forgotten people of the past.

On these islands the sounds of the sea are omnipresent. They blot out the memories of land. And each sea-sound is distinct from the others. In the old days each sound was a signal which could mean life or death. The poet Celia Thaxter who lived on the Shoals (as the islands are known locally) writes:

Each island, every isolated rock, has a rote of its own; and ears made delicate by listening in great and frequent peril can distinguish the bearings of each in a dense fog. The threatening speech of Duck Island's ledges, the swing of the wave over Halfway Rock, the touch of the ripple on the beach at Londoner's, the long and lazy breaker that is forever rolling below the lighthouse on White Island—all are distinct to the islander and indicate his whereabouts as clearly as if the sun were shining and no surrounding mist were striving to mislead him" (*Among the Isles of Shoals*, Boston, 1873).

The old-time islanders could take care of themselves in rough weather. But strangers weren't always so fortunate. In bygone days, shipwrecks were a commonplace. Often during

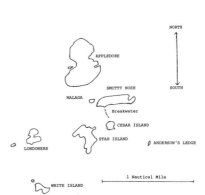

The Isles of Shoals

the gales of winter, vessels driven by mountainous seas would founder on the rocks and pound themselves to pieces, hurling their crews ashore sometimes to die of exposure.

Captain Samuel Haley of Smutty Nose once had a grim experience of shipwreck. It was his custom to keep a candle burning all night in a window of his house facing the sea "for the relief of poor mariners in distress of weather." One stormy winter morning in 1809 he opened his door to find two corpses peacefully curled up in the snow. Two more lay nearby. During the night the Spanish bark *Sagunto* had smashed to pieces on the black cape at the end of the island. The survivors had crawled, dying, toward his friendly light, only to perish inches away from safety. He buried them on the spot. You may see their graves today.

The Hontvet house. *Photo courtesy of Mr. Emile Burn.*

Of course islands like these have their fanciful ghost stories. A girl is said to have been marooned on Appledore by pirates some two hundred and fifty years ago. She was in love with their captain. The mate was in love with *her*. The crew loved none of the three, so they dumped the girl ashore.

One hundred years later she returned to trouble the peace of mind of a susceptible male visitor. For several nights he saw her standing on the rocks, arms outstretched and long black hair tumbling over her shoulders. She gazed fixedly out to sea and cried, "He *shall* come back!" One night she didn't appear. For a while the visitor saw her no more. Then came a fierce gale—waves pounding and wind shrieking, spray driving over the rocks. In the dead of night he woke with the knowledge that she was watching him. He could see nothing in the darkness. Then through the crash and roar of the gale he heard her wild and ringing laughter.

The Shoals were discovered by John Smith in 1614. He noted the teeming schools of mackerel, cod, hake, and haddock and predicted prosperity (for people, not for the fish). His prediction came true. By the mid-seventeenth century the Shoals were the site of one of the most important towns of New England. The town did a thriving business in dried fish with such remote places as Amsterdam and Bilbao and made money. Often as many as six full-rigged ships rode at anchor off the shore of Smutty Nose. The town had a church and meetinghouse, several taverns, a court that sat "for all ye western isles," and a finishing school for young ladies.

The American Revolution put an end to all this magnificence. The respectable part of the population dispersed to the mainland. Only the ne'er-do-well element remained and soon sank into brawling drunkenness and lewdness. In a couple of generations their descendants had died out, and the day of the "Shoalers" was over.

Only a handful of people were

167

White Island Light seen from Star Island. *Photo by James Wentz.*

living on the Shoals in March of 1873: the lighthouse keepers on White Island, Celia Thaxter on Appledore, some carpenters building a summer hotel on Star Island, and a few fishermen.

The sole inhabitants of Smutty Nose were a family of Norwegians. There were John Hontvet and his wife Maren, his brother Matthew, Maren's sister Karen Christensen, and her brother Ivan with his bride Anethe.

John Hontvet was a hard working, God fearing fisherman in his mid thirties; proud, taciturn, and practical. His wife Maren was a bustling and energetic little woman of cheerful disposition.

Karen was a quiet and self-effacing maiden of thirty, melancholy from the loss of a lover in the old country. For a while she had been a domestic in Celia Thaxter's home on Appledore, and the young American matron often thought what a charming picture Karen presented, sitting hours at the spinning wheel, flaxen hair falling over her shoulders, eyes gazing into a lost vision of the past.

Ivan and Anethe were normal and uncomplicated young people, frolicsome, full of the joy of life, much in love.

About John Hontvet's brother Matthew nothing is known.

The family lived in a little frame house of unpainted clapboard of the type you may see today on any back-country road in New England. It stood on top of a windswept knoll open to the elements. Near the house was a well that was to play a grisly part in the crime that followed. Nearby was a cove edged by purplish mussel shells, and here the men moored a schooner called the *Clara Bella*. They fished from this schooner, drawing their trawls near the Shoals and selling the catch in Portsmouth.

When they were away fishing the three women were alone on the island, except for Maren's little dog Ringe.

They had a friend named Louis Wagner. He was an uneducated

The cape at the end of Smutty Nose. *Photo by James Wentz.*

German fisherman of twenty-eight, an immigrant of about two years' standing. At first he had lived in sailors' flophouses in Boston and Portsmouth, but in 1872 he had tried fishing on his own from Star Island without any luck. For the balance of that year the Hontvets had taken him into their home, giving him his food, treating him as one of the family. For a while he was ill, and the women nursed him through it.

He was a likeable fellow; blond and nordic, with the gentleness of manner that some big, hulking fellows have. He was believed to be simple and without guile.

In March 1873 he was living in a boarding house on Water Street in Portsmouth, out of work and hard up. He owed several weeks' rent. He subsisted on handouts, and was most vocal about it. Once he pointed to his torn shoes and said he must have money soon if he had to do murder

for it. On another occasion he said if he could get a boat and go out to the Shoals, he knew where he could find money enough. No one listened.

At daybreak on March 5th the three Norwegian fishermen put to sea in the *Clara Bella* to draw their trawls northeast of Smutty Nose. They intended to return in the evening, leave one man to stay with the women, then put in to Portsmouth.

But that afternoon they had a head wind back to the Shoals. By means of a local fisherman they spied in a dory, they sent word home that they would be away all night.

This was the first time they had left the women alone at night.

That evening they tied up at Rollins' wharf in Portsmouth. By chance they encountered Louis Wagner. He asked "You go back to the Shoals tonight?" They said no. John Hontvet explained that he and the others expected to work all night baiting

169

Another view of White Island Light. *Photo by James Wentz.*

trawls. Would Wagner help them? The latter agreed.

But he never showed up for work. Several times during the night John Hontvet made inquiries about his whereabouts, but to no avail. In the weeks to follow, no one in Portsmouth was found who had seen Wagner after nine that evening.

He had stolen a dory to row out to the Shoals.

To landsmen today such a feat will seem amazing, a six-mile row across a wintry ocean and then back again. But no one in Portsmouth in those days thought it remarkable. When the matter reached a court of law much later, several persons testified that they had done it themselves. John Hontvet had rowed "fifty or sixty times" from Portsmouth to Smutty Nose in about three hours. A longshoreman testified that he had rowed from the Piscataqua River (on which Portsmouth is situated) to the

Shoals in only one hour—he had started from the river mouth.

At nine o'clock on the evening of March 5th a fisherman had left his dory at the foot of Pickering Street. When he returned half an hour later, it was gone.

A swift running current carried Wagner three miles down the Piscataqua River, past Whale's Back Light, and out into the Atlantic. It was a cold, clear night. The moon was shining brightly. The stiff breeze of the day had fallen off, and not much sea was running—just enough to swing the dory's bow up and down. The lights of Newcastle fell away astern. Boone Island shone far to the northeast. And dead ahead, the beam of White Island Light at the Shoals flashed over six miles of ocean—a beacon that even a landlubber could not have missed.

He pulled up on the rocks of Smutty Nose at midnight, leaving

Louis Wagner. *Photo courtesy of Mr. Emile Burn.*

the dory well to the east of the Hontvet house. Then followed an hour of reconnoitering. His rubber boots were silent on the snow; but the moon lit up the whole archipelago like noontime, and he ducked behind the rocks where he could. Someone might be up and about. He peered across the water at Appledore and Star Islands. Darkness there. He peeped into the little cove, but the *Clara Bella* had not returned. The Hontvet house was dark and silent.

Finally he crept up to the house. The door was unlocked. It led into the kitchen and he entered. A piece of two-by-four lay on a table, and with this he barred the door into the next room—he imagined that the women were sleeping there.

The dog Ringe barked hoarsely.

"John! Is that you?" Karen had been sleeping in the kitchen, and in the darkness she thought the men had returned.

Maren and Anethe had been asleep in the next room. They woke and jumped out of bed. "What's the matter?" "John scared me," Karen cried.

Wagner picked up a chair and dealt Karen a savage blow. It missed, but it dislodged a clock over her bed which fell to the floor—it was found next morning, the hands pointing to seven minutes past one.

"John kills me! John kills me!"

Karen rose and staggered toward the inner door. The stick of two-by-four became dislodged and the door swung open. Maren dragged her sister inside and locked the door behind them. She urged Anethe to climb out the window and scream for help; someone on Star Island just might still be awake. Anethe climbed out the window, but her nerve failed: "I cannot make a sound," she whimpered.

A tall figure came around the corner of the house. An axe swung from his hand (the family had left it by the front door).

"Louis! Louis!" Anethe had recognized him. The moment was final. There was no further question that it was John. Months and even years of legal procedure were to follow; but Wagner's doom was sealed at this moment of recognition.

He buried the axe in Anethe's brain.

Maren screeched to her sister to fly with her. "I haven't the strength," Karen moaned. Maren hastily scrambled out a window giving on the rear of the house. The dog Ringe jumped out after her.

Her first thought was to flee to the henhouse and hide in its cellar. But she discarded the idea; it was too obvious. In this her reasoning was correct: next day Wagner's footprints were found in the snow all around the area. Then she thought of the cove; a boat might be at anchor, but there was none. Her last hope was flight in a direction where no help could possibly exist. With bare feet numb on the sharp rocks, clad only in a shawl, the little dog tripping her up, clawing her way through matted bushes—she fled toward the seaward end of the island and hid in a cove.

She heard screams from the house. Wagner had returned to the kitchen, broken in the bedroom door, and was methodically slaughtering Karen. He struck her with the axe until the handle broke. Then he strangled her with a scarf just to make sure she was dead. He dragged the body of Anethe into the house and wrapped a scarf around her neck too.

Then he calmly sat by the corpses of the two women he had murdered and ate a meal. After that, he took a basin and towel and went out to the well to try to wash some of the blood off his hands and clothing.

Now, if not sooner, the thought of his deadly peril must have entered

his mind. A witness had escaped and must be found. He searched for Maren in the outbuildings, the cove, all around the vicinity of the house (his footprints were found later in the snow, circling about for hundreds of yards)—and he had to give up. She was nowhere to be found.

The first part of his plan had gone wrong.

Then came the search for the money. He searched through boxes, trunks, suitcases, bureau drawers, and all he got was twenty dollars. The second part of his plan had gone wrong.

But the gods had played him a little prank. Hidden between two sheets at the bottom of a trunk was the sum of several hundred dollars in bills, worth many times more than that today. It was Hontvet's life savings. Wagner's bloody fingerprints were found on the very sheet on which the money reposed, but he missed it. It would have meant temporary wealth and probable escape. The third part of his plan had gone wrong.

He was a calm and phlegmatic man, but now he must have begun to panic. He had plunged his hands in blood for a pittance. In the darkest hour before dawn (the moon had gone under) he raced back to the mainland. He must have rowed frantically, the gallows chasing him across the miles of dark water.

With physical exhaustion had

come mental confusion. He began acting like a fool. He wandered about making damaging admissions to various persons, idly boarded a train for Boston, got a shave and haircut and a new suit (twenty dollars was worth lots more in those days), and was arrested while boasting to some doxies in a sailors' bar.

A curious legal situation developed. It now was discovered that the two northernmost of the Isles of Shoals belong to Maine, not to New Hampshire as had been supposed, so Wagner was brought to trial at Alfred, the seat of York County. The trial began on June 9th, 1873 and took nine days. No defense was possible. Wagner was convicted and sentenced to death, and after long litigation was finally hanged at the state penitentiary in Thomaston on June 25th, 1875.

Back on the morning of March 6th, 1873, Maren had crouched all night in a little cove hugging her dog to her for warmth. She wasn't far from where Wagner had pulled up his dory. She must have had a narrow escape when he left.

At six-thirty, streaks of light had appeared in the sky. She didn't dare move; the murderer might still be about. At seven came the sound of hammering from Star Island; the carpenters were at work on the hotel. She climbed a rock and gesticulated wildly, but they did not notice. Then, giving the house a wide berth, she stumbled to the part of the island nearest Appledore. Some children were playing before their parents' house on that island; she caught their attention.

Minutes later a boat pulled over. The men in it found a woman whose mind had gone. They took her to Appledore, where kindly folk nursed her back to mental health. Then John Hontvet took her to a new home in Portsmouth, where she was to spend the rest of her days.

About a year after the murder of his bride Ivan Christensen went back to Norway. Matthew went with him. John built a big schooner for fishing on the Newfoundland banks and prospered quite nicely.

You may visit the scene of the crime today, if you wish. The house has vanished. The islands are eternal: Duck Island's ledges with the surf booming over them, Appledore's weird-looking dikes of traprock, the coarse and treacherous plain of Smutty Nose—all the haunting beauty of this far off spot.

One trace of the crime does remain. It is the well at which Wagner tried to wash the blood from his hands.

Bar Harbor: A Resort is Born

by Richard A. Savage

In the spring of 1844 the famed Hudson River artist Thomas Cole lost a close friend to a fatal illness. Suddenly New York City pressed in upon him, and Cole knew that he must get away from the studio, the crowded streets, the noise. He needed to find some faraway place where he could gather his thoughts in relative peace and tranquility. He no doubt considered the White Mountains of New Hampshire, for he had been there often to sketch and paint, sometimes with his friend and colleague Henry Pratt, a Maine native. Cole now sought out Pratt, and the two men at length decided to journey to what was for Cole virgin territory, the Maine coast. More specifically, their destination was Mount Desert Island which for several years had been an out-of-the-way summer resort for a few hardy Bostonians. It was a happy choice.

Vacationing Bostonians generally boarded at Southwest Harbor, Mount Desert's largest town, but even Southwest Harbor, with its few shops, yachts, and fishing vessels, was too busy a place to suit Cole and Pratt. They proceeded to the sparsely populated eastern shore of the island. There they found lodging at the rustic "Lynam Homestead" on ruggedly beautiful Schooner Head near the hamlet of Bar Harbor. John Lynam's family home seems to have been the only "boarding house" near Bar Harbor in the mid-1840's, the Lynams having found it worthwhile to supplement their meagre income by "takin' in" what few resorters meandered past. As far as Cole and Pratt were concerned, the Lynams did their job well.

Cole was captivated by the charm and beauty of Mount Desert. Not only at Schooner Head but elsewhere in and around Bar Harbor he found a variety of scenes to sketch in pen and pencil. A few of these sketches soon became widely exhibited oils, and it was through these paintings that Bar Harbor first came to public notice. Thomas Cole had, in the language of resorts, "discovered" Bar Harbor, and through his work this "discovery" was unveiled to New England and the nation.

Panorama of the mountains at Bar Harbor, c. 1900. *Photo courtesy of the Bar Harbor Historical Society*

The talented Cole was popular throughout the East, notably in Boston: his patrons included such prominent New Yorkers as Luman Reed and William P. van Rensselaer. The artist also was a close friend of the influential poet, publisher, and journalist William Cullen Bryant, who did what he could to further Cole's career. With the major cities of the Northeast engaged in a race for cultural hegemony and with "art unions" and "artist fund societies" cropping up in every urban center, it was a good time to be an artist. The popularizing influence of artists never was greater. As many as a half-million people viewed Cole's canvasses at the New York Art Union, a substantial audience.

Cole produced his best Bar Harbor oil "Frenchman's Bay, Mount Desert Island, Maine" in 1845, the year following his visit, and he finished several other noteworthy works. Soon other artists followed—Thomas Doughty, Benjamin Campney, John Kensett, and the noted marine artist Fitz Hugh Lane, among others. Lane's "View of Bar Harbor and Mount Desert Mountains . . ." (1850) was yet another testimonial to the attractions of the island's eastern shore.

Cole's prize pupil Frederic Edwin Church visited Mount Desert in 1850 and liked it so much that he returned at least six times during a busy career. Church, the most popular artist of the day (Cole had died in 1848), produced numerous

175

Main Street in the early 1880's, Rodick House at far left. *Photo courtesy of the Bar Harbor Historical Society.*

successful oils that further publicized Bar Harbor and Mount Desert. Perhaps the two most effective were serene "Oil Sketch of Bar Harbor" and his powerful "Storm at Mount Desert."

Church in turn was followed to Bar Harbor by Charles Temple Dix and later by Albert Bierstadt, Church's major artistic rival in the 1860's. If one assumes its resort development as "good" rather than "bad," Bar Harbor was fortunate to have such talented men as its first publicists. As early as 1850 the first *steady* trickle of visitors to the village had begun, though there were as yet no hotels or even full-fledged boarding houses to receive them. Resorters stayed at John Lynam's humble "homestead," or at the Bar Harbor home of Albert Higgins, a prominent member of one of the hamlet's pioneering families.

Bar Harbor's resort development was given further impetus when in

1853 Professor Alexander Bache, Director of the United States Coast Survey, selected Green Mountain (now Cadillac) near Bar Harbor as a triangulation point for the coast survey project. As useful as was the national exposure Bar Harbor received through the very existence of the survey, even more important was Bache's association with the project. A grandson of Benjamin Franklin, Philadelphian Bache was as prominent socially as he was renowned among his fellow scientists. Thus a good many eminent Philadelphians soon came to know of Bar Harbor and Mount Desert, making it clear that the Bostonians soon would have to share their retreat.

Bache also was the intimate friend of Louis Agassiz, Harvard's famed geologist, and the two men took several professional trips along the New England coast on Coast Survey vessels. Agassiz developed an interest in Maine rock formations and was eager to tour the coast later at a more leisurely pace. Mount Desert was among the places that impressed him.

Throughout the 1850's the number of Bar Harbor resorters rapidly increased, putting a severe strain on local facilities. By the mid-fifties Higgins, Lynam (and perhaps one or two others) no longer could accommodate the growing number of people who sought lodging at Bar Harbor. Church expressed bewilderment that "some shrewd Bostonian" had not yet recognized the hamlet's resort potential. But apparently none had. Most resorters were compelled to stay at Southwest Harbor and travel to Bar Harbor and its environs by buckboard (for the scenery of course), a long and uncomfortable trip. Southwest Harbor had become a moderately successful resort because a few families had seen the economic potential of resort enterprise, and it was left for Bar Harborites to learn from this example. The first crisis in the growth of a resort was at hand.

This initial challenge was met in 1855 when Tobias Roberts, a prominent villager, opened the Agamont House, Bar Harbor's first hotel. His foresight in building the hotel was a key to Bar Harbor's future development. Someone had to take advantage of the opportunity made possible in part by the work of the artists, in part by the handiwork of the Creator, and, one must assume, in part by the cooking and general good cheer of Mrs. Lynam and Mrs. Higgins. It may be that Roberts' shabby white wooden structure, situated by the sea on a treeless plot of rocky ground, was not deserving of the appellation "hotel"; but the Agamont was *meant* to be a hotel in the best sense of the word and this is what is important. The vital first step toward building a resort had been taken, and while the accommodations admittedly were crude, this mattered little to the early resorters.

Three years after Roberts had opened the now busy Agamont, Robert Carter, the New York *Tribune's* Washington correspondent, visited Bar Harbor aboard the chartered sloop *Helen.* Carter's party stopped first at Southwest Harbor (". . . the place of most resort on the island"), thence to Bar Harbor (". . . to be near the finest scenery"). They stayed at the Agamont where ". . . we found excellent quarters."

Upon his return to New York, Carter wrote about his trip for the *Tribune.* A few years later the articles were published in book form: for the first time Bar Harbor received notice in a popular narrative. Like the artists before him, Carter was impressed, though not uncritically, by the beauties of Mount Desert:

Newport House, 1881. *Photo courtesy of the Bar Harbor Historical Society.*

Of late years, Mount Desert has become a favorite resort for artists and for seaside summer loungers. But it needs the hand of cultivated taste for the full development of its matchless natural beauties.... Half a century of judicious clearing ... would make this island ... a place of pilgrimage and refuge ... to all lovers of the beautiful and sublime in nature.

There was an element of prophecy in Carter's words.

The summer of Carter's voyage, Ephraim Alley opened the Mountain House, giving Bar Harbor two hotels. Then Daniel Brewer built the Green Mountain House on the mountaintop near the Coast Survey headquarters. While the summit was some distance from Bar Harbor village, Brewer had a steady business from resorters who had climbed the mountain and then were either unable or unwilling to make the long downward trek to Bar Harbor at nightfall. They enjoyed the Green Mountain House.

In the fall of 1864 Agassiz at last returned to Mount Desert. He came primarily to study glacial formations, but also as a tonic for his health. Writing in the influential *Atlantic Monthly*, he compared the scenery of Mount Desert to that of the Scandinavia he so deeply loved. Since Agassiz was prominent in Boston society, his favorable pronouncements had a positive effect on the resort's growth. One of Agassiz's pupils Nathan Shaler also visited the island and later wrote extensively on the island's geology. His kind words did Bar Harbor and Mount Desert no harm.

Bar Harbor's traditional occupations rapidly gave way to the resort trades. Retired sea-captain James Hamor found it propitious to abandon shipbuilding and erect the Hamor House (1864), thus becoming the resort's fourth hotelier. Two years later David Rodick left his fishing business and, with his sons, built a boarding house in Bar Harbor. There was more than enough business for all the early proprietors, even during the Civil War years.

"Shore Acres," built for Dr. Hasket Derby, 1881. *Photo courtesy of the Bar Harbor Historical Society.*

The resorters who made such ventures both possible and necessary came from Boston, New York, Philadelphia, Washington, D.C., New Haven, Providence, Peoria, Chicago, and from as far away as Texas and California. These visitors became important Bar Harbor "boosters"; although it is difficult to measure with precision, word-of-mouth advertising clearly has a profound impact on resort development. Good things were being said about Bar Harbor, and the resort fast was becoming a popular success. By the mid-sixties Bar Harbor was, without dispute, undergoing remarkable social and economic change.

Bar Harbor was popular in its formative years because it was "rustic." The artists and the intellectuals who followed them sought escape from the stifling routine of America's fast-growing cities. These resorters were in effect "going back to nature." They called themselves "rusticators," and they sought pleasant, healthful, uncrowded surroundings. They did not demand luxury, fortunately, nor did they seek the artificial trappings of more formal "Society." Primitive Mount Desert filled their needs. And if Bar Harbor was a bit backward, even by the rusticators' tolerant standards, progress *was* being made, thanks largely to Tobias Roberts. Roberts exemplified a new and adventuresome spirit that soon captured the imaginations of others among the local inhabitants. He built a wharf at Bar Harbor, no doubt in hopes of attracting regular visits from the Mount Desert steamboat which still stopped only at Southwest Harbor; and by 1860 he had added bowling alleys and a "billiard saloon" to his other enterprises which included a fish market and general store. Roberts also lent money to Bar Harborites as the need arose, there being as yet no bank in town.

Resort life at Mount Desert in the 1850's is vividly portrayed in the

Minot and Weld cottages, c. 1900. *Photo courtesy of the Bar Harbor Historical Society.*

unpublished "log book" of New York lawyer Charles Tracy, and this picture would hold true at least through the late sixties. In 1855 Tracy had accompanied Church to Mount Desert, where the men hiked, daily climbed mountains, fished, picked blueberries and raspberries, and, on Sundays, attended church. Church services, according to Tracy, were "in keeping with the Puritan tradition," that is to say *long*, with a strategically placed intermission. Evenings were spent at home playing charades, dancing, fiddling, or singing to the accompaniment of Tracy's piano which had been shipped by rail and steamer all the way from New York.

Tracy, his family, and Church stayed at Somesville, a few miles from Bar Harbor, but they journeyed to Bar Harbor on occasion, once staying overnight at the new Agamont. Unfortunately the village of Bar Harbor itself presented a most unattractive visage in the mid-fifties, however beautiful the surrounding countryside. The Agamont was unimpressive, and there were no shops of significance.

Streets were few in number, narrow, rutted, and, when it rained, became seas of mud. The "hand of cultivated taste," as Carter phrased it, was most conspicuous by its absence. "Toby" Roberts and other local entrepreneurs still had a long road to hoe.

At Somesville things were a bit livelier, thanks to Tracy. Before returning to New York in late summer, the lawyer invited several island residents to a farewell party, and such parties being few and far between on Mount Desert, the turnout was predictably good. Tracy proved an able host, offering an abundance of good food to complement the main course of lobster salad. The customary home entertainments were provided, and dancing continued well into the night. The last guests did not depart for Bar Harbor until the unheard of hour of two o'clock A.M. The next day, presumably fully recovered from the festivities, Tracy and family boarded the little steamer *Rockland* at Southwest Harbor for the first leg of the return trip, leaving Mount Desert a

"Casa Par Niente," built for Wm. Rice, 1882. *Photo courtesy of the Bar Harbor Historical Society.*

little less moribund than they had found it. And once back in the Empire State, the Tracys would tell their friends and acquaintances of that distant Maine island, while Church would again paint.

Tracy's young daughter Frances, a minor figure in the "log book," had an unbounded love for Mount Desert. She later became the second wife of the renowned John Pierpont Morgan, and in 1875 she returned to Mount Desert (this time to Bar Harbor) accompanied by her wealthy husband. J. P. Morgan thus became the first of America's great financiers to place his seal of approval on the resort. He would return many times. But in the late 1860's the rich had not yet discovered Bar Harbor (in the sense of utilizing it), in part because they still were occupied making their millions, and in part because of the proximity of Newport and other resorts to the population centers of

the East. Suffice it to say that the early Mount Desert rusticators were a homogeneous group of artists, scholars, scientists, writers, and an occasional merchant who loved the beauty of coastal Maine.

The sixties brought few changes in the basic social routine for most resorters, but the groundwork slowly was being laid for a new era. There was increasingly more social and cultural activity for those so inclined. Occasional amateur theatrical performances were given at Bar Harbor, and there were numerous concerts by touring glee clubs and choruses. Excursion steamers now carried sightseers across Frenchman's Bay to the hamlets and fishing villages of Sorrento, Winter Harbor, Prospect Harbor, and Grindstone—future resorts all. In August 1867 the entire Boston Yacht Club fleet anchored in the harbor, and Bar Harbor's first grand ball was held at the brand

Alpheus Hardy's cottage, 1867. *Photo courtesy of the Bar Harbor Historical Society.*

new Rodick House in honor of Fleet Commodore Follett. Significantly, even the New York *Times* took notice of the successful affair.

Still resorters spent most of their time hiking, boating, and picnicking. The hike up Green Mountain remained popular, and rowing on Eagle Lake at the foot of Green also was a favorite pastime. Unfortunately for would-be sailors, the lake's rental boats were in ill repair and so few in number that reservations often were necessary. These deficiencies notwithstanding, some local entrepreneur obviously recognized a market to be exploited and had proceeded to do so. Such an example of initiative and ingenuity, at least at this early stage of Bar Harbor's development, surely must offset the operation's shortcomings.

For many, the Bar Harbor of the 1860's was far *too* rustic and too crude to serve as a place of resort. Philadelphia's Dr. Silas Weir Mitchell is a case in point. The noted neurologist, novelist, and social "lion" first visited Bar Harbor in 1866, while recuperating from a nervous breakdown precipitated by several years of treating Civil War casualties. Like Cole, Church, and the others, he was attracted by the beauty and serenity of Mount Desert. But Mitchell found it no place to live for the summer season. He was appalled by what he deemed an unforgiveable dearth of the simple amenities of life; largely for this reason, he spent the following summers in the more refined (some would say more artificial and affected) atmosphere of Newport.

No doubt similar opinions were commonplace. Bar Harbor still had little appeal for aristocrats of the Newport variety and certainly was not ready for them. Those used to the more structured social life of the city and "watering places" found Bar Harbor's social routine too informal and too "low brow" to suit them; and what "Society" there was, appeared unbearably democratic by Newport standards. An informal propriety was the best one could hope for at Bar Harbor, and even this was sometimes lacking. So Bar Harbor remained, temporarily, the refuge of rusticators.

Rodick House when all additions were completed in 1882. *Photo courtesy of the Bar Harbor Historical Society.*

By 1870 there were sixteen hotels in town, all owned by natives of Bar Harbor and vicinity. But resort activity was not centered entirely upon the hotels. Shortly after the war's end another and significant trend became evident when non-residents at last began to invest in Bar Harbor's future. Alpheus Hardy, a prominent Boston merchant and trustee of the Montgomery Sears estate, led the movement. In 1867 Hardy left his boarding house and, for the sum of $300, purchased a desirable plot of land at Bar Harbor where he constructed a private "cottage." In the parlance of France's Old Régime, after Hardy—the deluge.

Land prices were low, and those boarders who yearned for more privacy than the thin-walled hotels could provide, hastened to follow Hardy's lead. By 1869 more than a dozen non-residents owned property locally, while many already were building cottages.

Most of the early cottagers were Bostonians, and logically so. New Yorkers still treasured Newport, while Bar Harbor was a long ride from Philadelphia, Washington, and Baltimore. Besides Hardy, Boston contributed the Minots, Welds, Dorrs, and Derbys—all old established families. Dr. Hasket Derby, for example, was co-founder of the American Ophthalmological Society and a member of four prestigious Boston clubs. The lone New Yorker among the early cottagers was Gouverneur Ogden, Assistant Director of the Coast and Geodetic Survey and member of the illustrious New York clan.

At first, of course, the number of cottages remained small, and the hotels dominated Bar Harbor's social life until the early eighties. Twenty eventful years passed before the social, if not the numerical, supremacy of the cottagers was established. But the homes of Hardy and the others, however modest they may appear in retrospect, were a beginning, and the construction

Bay View Hotel, built 1869.
*Photo courtesy of the Bar Harbor
Historical Society.*

of these first cottages was a significant milestone—perhaps better, watershed—in Bar Harbor's resort development. A few resorters at least now were establishing roots.

The growth of the resort was further enhanced by the increasing accessibility of Bar Harbor and Mount Desert. Beginning in the 1830's there was regular steamboat service between Boston, Portland, Rockland, and Bangor, and in 1856 service was started between Portland and New York (railroad to Providence or Boston, then steamer to Portland). The railroad was extended to Portland in 1842, to Bath in 1850, and to Bangor in 1857. Thus resorters had several means of travel to and from the state. Commercially speaking, coastal Maine was fortunate to be connected to the great population centers of the East relatively early.

Travelers could go from New York, Boston, and Portland by rail or boat (or some combination) to Rockland where, after 1854, they could take the small, slow, but popular steamer *Rockland* to Southwest Harbor (as Church and Tracy had). Sometimes a steamer would run from Bangor to Mount Desert upon the arrival at Bangor of the Boston-Bangor boat of the Sanford Line, and a few hardy souls even took the stage from Bangor to Bar Harbor via Ellsworth, a long trip.

Water transportation to Mount Desert was disrupted by the Civil War when the government took both *Rockland* and her successor *T. F. Secor* for military use. The loss of these boats slowed the flood of visitors to Bar Harbor, but not catastrophically. And once the war was over, regular steamboat service was restored with significant additions. Captain Charles Deering was the moving force behind the creation of the Portland, Bar Harbor, and

Machias Steamboat Company, the first such concern to provide direct and reliable service to and from Bar Harbor. Service was inaugurated in 1868 by the sleek steamer *Lewiston*.

The steamers were a success because people wanted to visit Bar Harbor. And the arrival of the steamboats on a regular basis in turn inspired a burst of activity on the part of the townspeople. Both established proprietors and the newly arrived now could receive supplies by sea. Tobias Roberts was so hopeful that he built his second hotel, the Rockaway.

While the steamers were by no means the sole cause of the hotel boom, they provided a steady supply of lodgers and may well have made the construction of so many hotels and boarding houses feasible over the long term. By serving as freighters as well, the steamers clearly facilitated the expansion of the resort. Bar Harbor was well developed by the time the first direct train service was instituted in 1884.

As the decade of the sixties came to a close, Bar Harbor was fast becoming a full-fledged resort. A building boom engulfed the town. In 1869 alone, over a half million feet of lumber was delivered to Bar Harbor's waterfront, to be used primarily for hotel and cottage construction. It was evident that the will and desire to develop a resort, instilled by the diminutive Mr. Roberts, had inspired the imaginations of Bar Harborites. Farmers abandoned their fields and fishermen their nets to become involved in the resort trades. Ship carpenters became the builders of cottages and hotels. Other inhabitants became gardeners, caretakers, livery men, maids, cooks, and porters. Those who continued to farm and fish now supplied the cottages and hotel dining rooms.

Of course there remained serious problems to solve before the future would be secured, and there was surely no guarantee in 1870 that Bar Harbor one day would be the summer playground of the Vanderbilts, Morgans, Pulitzers, Stotesburys, Kents, and McLeans. Before it could become a "watering place" the resort had to acquire considerably more polish and refinement. And so it did, with moderate speed, but relentlessly. As the 1870's dawned, Bar Harbor's mandate was becoming increasingly clear.

Memory Lies Deep in the Ashfield Hills

by Ursula Toomey

Spring comes late to the Ashfield hills. Old maples which line the village street are just coming into leaf even though the month of May has passed and the day has arrived for Ashfield to do honor to the veterans of many wars who lie buried in the town's cemeteries. Ashfield is proud of its past and of the patriotism which inspired men in this picturesque village in the hills of western Massachusetts to fight in every United States war from the French and Indian wars to the conflict in Vietnam. And Ashfield remembers.

"Remember" was the name of the daughter of Richard Ellis, the first settler of Huntstown, as Ashfield was originally called. It was named for Captain Ephraim Hunt who, in 1690, set out from Weymouth as commander of a company which participated in a Canadian Expedition and the struggle called King William's War. When he and his men returned, they were given grants of land in the western part of the state, but none of the grantees settled in Huntstown. The name of the town was changed to Ashfield in 1764 when town boundaries were fixed, the name apparently supplied by the

Governor of Masschusetts and his Council. At that time Lord Thurlow of Ashfield, England, was in sympathy with the cause of the colonies, so it is possible that the name "Ashfield" was chosen to do him honor.

Ashfield's seven cemeteries indicate that the town was once populous and prosperous. On the main stagecoach route between Boston and Albany, its distinguished citizens built aristocratic houses and a meetinghouse with well proportioned steeple fashioned after a Christopher Wren design. Now the meetinghouse is the town hall where town officials, veterans, boy scouts, girl scouts, and citizens gather on Memorial Day to form a parade which proceeds to the cemeteries with flags and flowers for the graves of heroes.

"Remember James Coughlin?" asks a World War I veteran. "The parade doesn't seem right without him. Until he was over ninety years old he marched every year, the last local survivor of the Grand Army of the Republic. He fought under Colonel Pickett of Greenfield as a member of the 25th Regiment. After the Civil War he joined the navy and on the U. S. Sloop *Richmond* under Admiral Farragut traveled the seven seas. He was a lifelong friend of the famous admiral and his son, Loyall Farragut, who for many years had a summer home in Ashfield. It is still called "Mizzen Mast," the name it was given by Admiral Farragut's son, at whose suggestion James Coughlin came to Ashfield to make his home. It was lonely being the only one left. Now the old men are those who fought in World War I fifty years ago. Quite a few of them are in the parade today."

The color guard, composed of one man from each of the military services, marches by with flags flying. The band composed of Sanderson Academy students in smart red and white uniforms strikes up a martial tune and the parade moves briskly down the village street.

It is passing now the house where for many years lived George William Curtis, well known writer and editor of *Harper's Magazine*. He had come to Ashfield in 1864 to visit his friend Charles Eliot Norton and was so charmed by the quiet beauty of the village that he decided not only to spend his summers in this "paradise among the hills" but to make Ashfield his permanent residence. Professor Norton, at that time a member of the Harvard College faculty and associate editor of the *North American Review,* lived at the end of a well worn path across the meadow. The two literary friends were

Salute.

devoted to the interests of their adopted village. Disturbed that there was not a finer academy for the education of children in the town, they set about to raise funds and standards, and to expand the educational facilities of the modest school. For twenty-five years they promoted the "Academy dinners," which drew capacity audiences to hear such famous speakers as William Dean Howells, Charles Dudley Warner, William Whiting, James Russell Lowell, Joseph H. Choate, Booker T. Washington, Richard Henry Dana, and others too numerous to mention. Of course, Dr. G. Stanley Hall, who was born in Ashfield and was frequently called "Sanderson Academy's sample scholar," was a frequent speaker both before and after he became president of Clark University. Financially, the dinners saved the life of the Academy.

The villagers didn't always agree with Professor Norton's ideas, partic-

Norton House.

ularly when he tried to revive the European class of peasantry and suggested an appropriate costume for each type of trade or guild. This was heartily resented, as well as the suggestion that barbed wire fences be replaced by the more decorative stone walls. But the funds raised at the dinners, from lectures given by Mr. Curtis in larger cities, and from readings of the classics given by Professor Norton were gratefully received.

The two editors formed the library association, too, so that there was no longer need to charge Austin Lilly three cents for "dirt in Boswell's Life of Johnson." "Dirt in the Life of Washington" came higher, for Eli Eldridge, Jr., paid twelve cents. James Russell Lowell, a frequent visitor at the home of Professor Norton, helped to expand the services of the library. He became so engrossed in making it a superior library that in 1885, when he was United States Minister to England,

he bought a site for a summer residence. Soon after Mrs. Lowell died and the Ambassador, deciding to remain in England, cancelled plans for his new home.

Banners rippling in the breeze, the procession enters the Plains Cemetery. Boy scouts assist members of the American Legion in placing flags on the graves of veterans, and Girl Scout Brownies distribute sprays and red poppies. Kindergarten children, led by their collie mascot, place bouquets of red tulips at the foot of the stone marking the grave of Amanda Ferry Hall. The granddaughter of Thomas White, Esquire, who was an esteemed citizen of Ashfield in the late eighteenth century, Mrs. Hall returned to spend her last years in the White Homestead. Sitting in the garden pergola topped by a weather vane carved to represent the Angel Gabriel blowing his horn into the four winds, she liked to reminisce aloud about the early days when her father held court in the summer kitchen, settling the disputes of his neighbors.

She often told how Mary Lyon, who lived in Buckland only a fraction of a mile from the much disputed Ashfield boundary, came to the new academy, the first high school in this part of the state, anxious to continue her education. But she could not be enrolled since she was not a citizen of the town. Mrs. Hall's grandfather, Thomas

White, whose imposing federal mansion built in 1790 still stands on the main street, took her into his home. Here she lived during her academy days sharing a room with his daughter, Amanda. When Amanda was ready to go to the Byfield Female Seminary, her father, finding Mary Lyon in tears, bundled her into the spring board wagon for a two-days' journey to the school where she was to secure her higher education.

Mary Lyon's first teaching job was in Ashfield's Steady Lane School where she taught fifty to seventy pupils ranging in age from five to twenty-one. Her pay was $5.50 a month with board, which meant that she boarded around at different homes, walking three to five miles from her temporary residence to the schoolhouse. In the evening she often helped the children of the family with their sums and organized spelling bees and debates for the adults of the village. In later years Mary Lyon often recalled the excitement generated by these informal debates. The schoolhouse was packed with participants and spectators when she or some community leader would present a controversial issue and open the subject for discussion, a wonderful training for holding office in town and state government. Mary Lyon liked to boast that her boys could hold their own in the state legislature in competition with

Curtis House.

men who were Harvard, Williams, or Amherst college graduates.

"It was my mother, Amanda White, who married Mary Lyon's fiance, the Reverend William Ferry," Mrs. Hall would relate. "As you see, I am named for her. Amanda had led a most conservative life here in Ashfield and at the Byfield Female Seminary, but off she went with her missionary husband to Michigan, then a dangerous wilderness. In 1840 Mackinac was pioneer country, only a few colonies of lumbermen and their families. I was the first white baby to be born on the island and received the startled adulation of the Indians."

The story of the Reverend William Ferry's endless trials in establishing missions and in caring for his family, of his later becoming one of Michigan's wealthiest merchants, is one of those fabulous tales of the early history of our country. His son, Mrs. Hall's brother, Thomas W. Ferry, a member of Congress

Children decorating graves.

for four terms, was elected United States Senator from Michigan and served as president pro tem of the Senate in 1875, later becoming acting Vice-President of the United States. In this position he presided in place of President Grant at the opening of the great Philadelphia Centennial Exposition in 1876. Mementoes of his life at the White House during an eventful administration are numerous in the White Homestead at Ashfield.

The graves decorated, members of the procession gather around the war memorial at the entrance of the cemetery and stand with bowed heads as the Reverend Philip H. Steinmetz offers prayer. The honor guard fires a volley into the air, the harsh reverberations barely ended when the mournful sound of taps melts into the soft spring air. Long afterward, their echo resounds from the tall evergreens at the edge of the woodland.

Every year someone remembers to take to the Baptist Corner Cemetery bunches of white lilacs for the graves of Isaac Shepard and Aaron Lyon, the grandfather and father of Mary Lyon. This tiny cemetery is about five miles from Ashfield center, halfway to Buckland where Mary Lyon was born. What more fitting time for a pilgrimage to the birthplace of the founder of the first women's college in America, Mount Holyoke College, than on Memorial Day. A well kept sign directs the visitor "To Mary Lyon's Birthplace" as he leaves the black top road and starts to climb through the hills of Buckland on a dirt road. The pilgrim is not worried when the road deteriorates and burrows ever deeper into virgin forests. The new and shiny signs posted every mile or so lure him on with promise of a reward. The road ends abruptly in a farm yard, but another polished sign discloses that it is a "One Mile Walk to Mary Lyon's Birthplace."

Lacy branches of ancient trees meet over the woodland road; trillium and jack-in-the-pulpits are sticking their heads through the thick moss. It is spring, and the ground is soft and marshy. A brook has overflowed its banks and creates a barrier, but a plank left by woodcutters is moved to build a temporary bridge. Is this clearing the spot? There is no continuation of the road, no sign of habitation. A cellar hole? A bronze tablet? Nothing. All those fine signs leading the pilgrim on, but no marker at the end of the journey.

The farmer is of no assistance. Was that the right place? Is there a cellar hole or a tablet to mark the spot? "I never seen none," said the farmer. Disappointment may be somewhat alleviated by reading in *Picturesque Franklin,* published in 1891, the experience of Clifton H. Johnson in seeking Mary Lyon's birthplace. Clifton Johnson, the father of Roger, Arthur, and Captain Irving Johnson, has left a record in pictures and stories of life in the early days of Massachusetts.

I called at the village store and inquired about the Mary Lyon place having seen on a road below a sign pointing the way. The reply was that it was four miles to the spot and about the hilliest hardest road I had ever seen. When you get there you will find nothing but an old cellar hole filled with weeds up in a pasture. He called it about nineteen miles from nowhere.

The village store was a buzz of activity when the parade was ended. The old boys were gathered around the pot-bellied stove swapping yarns.

"Yes, sir, Josephus Crafts run this store until the day he died, and he lived to be a hundred. Knew how to run it too. Marshall Field who was born right down here in Conway used to come back every summer to see his old friend Crafts and discuss

Douglas Ward leads parade.

merchandising problems with him. Marshall 'ud come in the store, wander around looking over the stock on the shelves. Old Crafts never looked up from his ledger. Finally he'd say, 'Looks pretty big to you, don't it Marshall?' Wouldn't be surprised if Marshall Field got some of his best ideas right here in this store. One day he listened while Crafts told off a customer. Cy Howe's wife cum in asking for blue gingham. 'Ain't got none in stock,' snapped Crafts without mincing words. Sweet and nice like, she asks, 'When will you have some, Mr. Crafts?' 'I ain't aimin' to have no more. The dern stuff sells too fast. Can't keep it in stock.' With my own two eyes I see Marshall Field take out his notebook and write that one down."

"Remember when we used to sit out in front of Azel Packard's antique store when the sun was warm? One day I was leaning back

To Mary Lyon's birthplace.

give Azel fifteen dollars fur it. Wasn't wuth more'n two. Had a better one in my own kitchen. You should 'uv been around here when George Hall was alive and belonged to the rememberin' club. His great grandfather was 'Squire White who built that house right across the street. His mother kept a record of everything that happened around here and the whole history of her family. George could find most anything he wanted over in that house to help his memory. Rememberin' is more than a pastime around here, it's a challenge."

in my creaky chair when it split plumb down the middle. Had to

A feeble man can only see the farms that are fenced and tilled; the houses that are built. At the end of the town, he is at the end of the world. The strong man sees not only the actual but the possible houses and farms. His eye makes estates and villages as fast as the sun breeds clouds.

R. W. Emerson, *Journals*
(Modern Library Edition, 1960),
p. 290.